SPIRITUAL
ENTREPRENEURS

INNOVATORS IN MINISTRY

SPIRITUAL ENTREPRENEURS

6 Principles for Risking Renewal

MICHAEL SLAUGHTER
Edited by Herb Miller

INNOVATORS IN MINISTRY

ABINGDON PRESS
Nashville

SPIRITUAL ENTREPRENEURS:
6 PRINCIPLES FOR RISKING RENEWAL

Copyright © 1994, 1995, by Michael Slaughter

Formerly published as *Beyond Playing Church: A Christ-Centered Environment for Church Renewal* (ISBN 0-917851-78-1) (Anderson, Ind.: Bristol House, Ltd.)

Library of Congress Cataloging-in-Publication Data

Slaughter, Michael.
    Spiritual entrepreneurs: 6 principles for risking renewal/
Michael Slaughter.
        p.   cm.—(Innovators in ministry)
    Rev. ed. of Beyond playing church. 1994.
    Includes bibliographical references (p.   ).
    ISBN 0-687-00799-2 (pbk.: alk. paper)
        1. Church renewal—United States—Case studies.   2. Ginghamsburg
United Methodist Church (Dayton, Ohio)   3. Church growth.
    I. Beyond playing church.   II. Title.   III. Series.
    BV600.2.S562   1995
    269—dc20   95-23064

99 00 01 02 03 04 — 10 9 8 7

MANUFACTURED IN THE UNITED STATES OF AMERICA

To
Carolyn, Kristen, and Jonathan—
"Gifts from God for the Journey"

Acknowledgments

My deep appreciation goes to Cheryl Haerer, who, for almost five years, has worked diligently on this project and the video series "First Love." Her research, administrative and word processing skills, prayer, and friendship have made the completion of this book possible. My thanks too to Elmo Flory for proofreading the manuscript and giving valuable suggestions.

I am indebted to Len Sweet and the others at United Seminary who have surrounded my life and encouraged the initial work. And I will be forever grateful to the people of Ginghamsburg Church, past and present, who have thrown gasoline on my burning bush along the way.

FOREWORD

Coffee conversations among pastors often affirm the value of organizing small groups that involve many of their churchs' members in Bible study, prayer, and sharing. Few churches, however, actually hit that target. The typical congregation involves fewer than 10 percent of its members in such groups.

For Michael Slaughter, this much-discussed but seldom-implemented "wave of the future" is past history and present reality. During the last fifteen years, his rural United Methodist congregation twenty miles from Dayton, Ohio, grew from an average of 90 to 2,100 worship attenders in four services each week (62 percent increase in the last three years.) The "meta-church" model (in which most members participate in a small group) helped that to happen. Author Frederich Buechner has said that the story of any one of us is in some measure the story of us all. Few leaders can say that about this church's story, but many will see in it something of what they would like to become.

Calling his approach an "applied theology of church re-newal," Slaughter describes the underlying theological foundation on which this "small-group church" developed. He sketches some of the how-to-do-it. Primarily, however, he concentrates on the empowering "why" behind this small-group system and its magnetic attraction ability.

In the history of idea invention and application, few people are innovators (creating something genuinely new). Some are early adopters. Still others are part of the early majority. Then come the later majority and the laggards. The intransigents prefer to die rather than change, and they usually do.

Fewer than 1 percent of church leaders are genuine innovators. But Slaughter's thoughts can help many forward thinkers to join the small-group "wave of the future."

—Herb Miller, Lubbock, Texas

CONTENTS

INTRODUCTION

The Christ-Centered Church

It was Super Bowl Sunday. After preaching three morning services and grabbing a quick bite to eat, I reluctantly got into my car to drive a couple of hours across the state to a sleepy county-seat town, to speak at another Protestant church. As I traveled through rural Ohio that bright, crisp, January afternoon, my mind was traveling also, considering all the possibilities of the evening to come. Surely, when this special Family Night had been planned five months earlier, the organizers had not realized that it would be in direct competition with the Super Bowl. They would be lucky to have 20 to 30 people present, and probably no one under the age of 40. I had even dressed down for the occasion, slipping into a comfortable sweater and slacks before leaving home.

When I arrived at the church about half an hour early, I was greeted by Marilyn and her husband Dave, who were organizing this family event. They were very enthusiastic about the possibilities. Marilyn expressed concern about the potential conflict with the football game, but felt Christ had a special purpose for the evening. They had creatively played up the Super Bowl theme and planned to begin the evening with a "Super Bowl Chili Supper."

As the fellowship hall began to fill, several people gathered around a TV to watch pregame events, while others chatted with friends. I was surprised that so many had turned out for the supper and wondered how many would leave immediately afterward, to make it home in time for the kickoff. A contemporary Christian group sang during the dinner, and several youth from the church who had formed a music group shared two original songs. The people really seemed to be enjoying themselves!

When it was time for me to speak, I noticed that no one was leaving. In fact, two new groups were just arriving from other local churches, and the hosts began setting up extra chairs. I had expected the Super Bowl to be a major detraction, but the fellowship hall was filled with old and young alike, eager to experience the renewing power of Jesus Christ.

As I looked around the room I thought to myself, "Surely these people have something else to do on Sunday evening." People are just plain physically, mentally, and spiritually exhausted, trying to keep up the pace of raising children and paying bills. With approximately 70 percent of the women born after 1946 working outside the home, when we *do* get home, we want to stay there. The video market and pizza-delivery industry flourish because of our baby-boomer tendency to "cocoon" in the security of our homes.

I had expected distraction and sparse attendance. But I found hunger, enthusiasm, and personal expressions of a new purpose, discovered through a relationship with Jesus Christ. The people of God have experienced enough games. On this Super Bowl evening, they were demonstrating a deep inner longing to make their lives count for a purpose greater than themselves. The same transforming power of God that I see working in the lives of my brothers and sisters at Ginghamsburg, I could see in the faces of these people. They were longing for a deeper experience of God.

As I drove home that night, I could not help thinking about what was happening in my denomination. Many of our vital signs and statistics indicate that we are a dying church, with a graying membership and declining rolls. But wait—I see other signs! As I share the Ginghamsburg story, I see enthusiasm and desire that can't be measured by statistics alone.

As I travel to churches across the country, I see evidence of renewed hunger for a living faith. I see people who are tired of playing church and are trying to find a way to *be* the church. Signs indicate that people have a renewed interest in the Word and the world. I hear from people who are longing for a deeper experience of God's Spirit. New Sunday school classes and Bible study groups are starting. Unchurched people are visiting our churches with refreshing openness. Pastors are talking about ministry, not maintenance. Lay people are going on the offensive, organizing small-group fellowships and outreach ministries. Bishops are discussing vital congregations and the development of faithful disciples as being the priority of the church. Stale mission statements are growing into challenging vision statements. There are islands of health and hope, where the church seems to be focusing on relationships more than on structure and organization. There is growing interest in the sacrament, and more and more of our people are boldly telling others about the transforming power of Jesus Christ in their lives.

Could it be . . . I thought to myself as I drove home through the clear winter night . . . that we are standing on the edge of a great spiritual awakening?

The Story of Ginghamsburg Church

My wife and I were returning to the office after a late lunch. As I turned into the parking lot of the patchwork campus of Ginghamsburg Church, I remarked to Carolyn, "This is truly a miracle. Look at this place. It's an eyesore! With the corn field, gravel parking lots, rusty garbage bins, and the mobile trailers that we use for classrooms, it looks more like a used-trailer lot than church grounds." More than once we have had to corral the neighbor's cows in the parking lot.

According to some church-growth experts, growth never should have occurred here. Our campus has been located in the same non-highly-visible location since 1876. There are three small buildings and four trailers. Most of our parking space is unpaved farm land.

Ginghamsburg is a small blip in the road, with approximately twenty houses. Tipp City, our mailing address, about four miles away, has a population of 7,000. Ginghamsburg is "urbanized country." By most accounts this is definitely a nonchurch-growth environment. And yet Ginghamsburg has grown to be the largest United Methodist church in Ohio, in the area of worship, Sunday school attendance, size of staff, and budget.

Ginghamsburg Church has a history that is fairly typical of many smaller mainstream denomination churches across the country. It was founded in 1863; the small brick and frame building where we worshiped until 1984 was built in 1876. Through the years, the membership flitted between 80 and 120, while the worship attendance ranged between 20 and 90. Most pastors stayed two to three years; the longest pastorate prior to my coming lasted five years.

The average attendance in the fall of 1974 was hovering around 20, and the annual income of the church was between $5,000 and $6,000. The people were struggling to pay the utility bills and the student pastor's salary. As the church clearly was in the grasp of institutional death, the district superintendent had offered the people one last opportunity before the doors of the church were to be permanently closed. He sent Jim Worley, a student at United Theological Seminary, to Ginghamsburg.

Jim did two things: He began telling the people about his personal experience with Jesus Christ, and he taught about the church's need to be a covenant community of radical love. Everything the church did needed to be centered around a commitment to the person of Jesus Christ, within the context of a loving, supportive fellowship.

Under Jim's leadership, the people began to meet together every Thursday night for a potluck supper. One Saturday night each month, they met in different homes. They called this meeting JOY (for *J*esus, *O*thers, and *Y*ou), and encouraged one another to bring unchurched friends who could be supported by this fellowship. Much like the church described in the book of Acts, they not only held worship services in their small two-room facility, "they broke bread at home and ate their food with glad and generous hearts" (Acts 2:46).

By the time I was appointed to Ginghamsburg United Methodist Church in April of 1979, the worship attendance had grown to 90 people on Sunday morning, with approximately 65 in Sunday school and a membership of 137. The annual budget was $27,000.

Fifteen years later, our weekend worship attendance averages close to 1,500, with more than 1,100 in educational experiences and 1,600 in small groups. Twenty-five hundred people would identify Ginghamsburg as their church home, but because of our membership standard, the figure drops to 900. The total income in 1994 was $2.2 million. We currently have more than 30 paid staff. Each week, an average of 40 families visit Ginghamsburg for the first time. The church supports a resale clothing store, a women's counseling center, a food pantry, a community-crisis ministry, a care and counseling center, three children's clubhouses in the inner city of Dayton and in Troy, Ohio, and a furniture warehouse in our local area. Those of us who have been experiencing this fresh wind of the Spirit are continually awed by God's work of grace.

We had begun this journey with some questions. Would people be turned off by new worship forms? Would a clear focus on Jesus as Lord and a tougher membership standard drive people away? We did lose about thirty of the original church members, and the loss was painful. Yet we heard the voice of Christ call us forward to risk the unknown, and the people were willing to risk doing things a new way.

The following graph indicates worship attendance, Sunday school attendance, and membership patterns since 1978.

At my denomination's governing conference in Baltimore in 1984, delegates adopted the ambitious goal of doubling the membership of the entire church to 20 million by 1992. Not only did we not reach that goal by 1992, but the church has continued to decline at the rate of more than a thousand members a week.[1] Needless to say, much attention has been given lately to growing churches. The emphasis on church growth is matched only by the flood of literature on the subject. Space needs, staffing, parking, promotion, calling programs, and small-group ministry—all get ample attention. *But techniques must never be the focus of growth!* The emphasis should never be placed on container over content, or task over spirit.

I have been given many opportunities during the last few years to share Ginghamsburg's story in conference, district, and local church meetings across my denomination. Many times, I have had the feeling that people were expecting me to share a list of things to do, or programs to try, so that their churches could experience growth like that at Ginghamsburg Church.

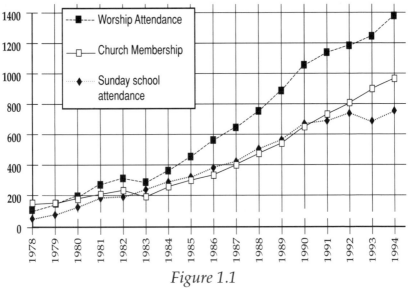

Figure 1.1

When I really began to look closely at what was happening at Ginghamsburg Church, however, I could not link the main causes of growth with any specific techniques. In some cases, we grew in spite of weak techniques. Growth seemed to be directly related to a work of the Spirit, rather than to our efforts alone. In some instances, growth has meant allowing God to take us in directions we really hadn't planned on going.

What I *was* able to identify, however, was a theology of renewal that had prepared our people for the transforming work of God's Spirit. True renewal has more to do with theology than with techniques. Techniques can be useful as tools to manage ministry, but should never become goals in themselves. Techniques need to have a solid theological foundation. They can be useful for getting people into a church, but the people won't stay unless they find spiritual authenticity. Advertising can generate customer traffic, but only the Spirit can transform human lives.

What Is Renewal Theology?

Each great awakening through nearly two thousand years of church history has employed different techniques. Altar calls, concerts of prayer, inquiry meetings, camp meetings, Wednesday-night services, men's breakfasts, women's organizations, small-group meetings, and a vast array of liturgical forms have helped carry the gospel message to diverse cultures. Church-growth techniques change with cultures and historical time periods, but an identifiable renewal theology has been universal to every revitalization throughout the history of the church.

In Ezekiel 37, the prophet is led by the Spirit of God into a valley of dry bones—bones that represented life from another time. A very significant question is asked: "Can these bones live?" (Ezek. 37:3) Can there be life again, where there is now death and decay? Is total transformation possible? Can dry institutions be transformed into vital movements?

> "Thus says the LORD GOD to these bones: I will cause breath to enter you, and you shall live. I will lay sinews on you, and will cause flesh to come upon you, and cover you with skin, and put breath in you, and you shall live . . . ."
> I prophesied as he commanded me, and the breath came into

them, and they lived, and stood on their feet, a vast multitude.
(Ezek. 37:5-6, 10)

The prophetic message from God opens God's people to the
Spirit of revitalization. It is a transforming work of the Spirit
that turns dry bones into the living body of Christ and mobilizes a vast army of reformers. Renewal is God-breathed, not
program planned!

The church in Ephesus could have been considered successful in many areas. It was a hardworking church that believed in
practicing what it preached. The people were known for their
good deeds and sound doctrine. When the going got tough,
they did not quit. The Christians at Ephesus were committed
to the work of the church in both good times and bad, yet they
had one critical flaw. The people had forsaken their first love.
They had become so busy doing the work of the Lord that they
had forgotten the Lord of the work. The messenger of the Lord
was calling them to repent and return to their first love (Rev.
2:1-7). The call was to remember first principles—the principles
of renewal.

During every period of renewal, the church has been universally committed to six theological principles:[2]

1. **The Lordship Principle:** a clear focus on Jesus Christ as
   the object of faith.
2. **The Biblical Principle:** scriptural truth as the primary
   source for what we believe and do.
3. **The Liturgical Principle:** discovery of new worship
   forms.
4. **The Covenant Principle:** commitment to the integrity
   of membership.
5. **The Priesthood Principle:** equipping the laity for ministry.
6. **The Leadership Principle:** spiritual entrepreneurship.

The church must have Christ-centered pastors and leaders.
They must be spiritual entrepreneurs who are committed to

these theological principles. Commitment to the prophetic message of these principles is essential for renewal to take place in the church today.

A Definition of Church Renewal

Church renewal is more than an increase in numbers and budgets. Many gimmicks can be employed to persuade people to come and sit in church pews. If our only goal were to increase attendance, we could even pay people to attend church. But until people become committed to being faithful to the will of God, their attendance is no more meaningful than membership in any other human organization or club. Church renewal consists of people in community with one another, dreaming God's vision, believing Christ's victory, and living out the Spirit's work. The evidence of renewal will be seen in transformed lives.

A Mother's Story

"Mom, being around Mike now is like, well, almost like having a new brother."

As I looked at our youngest son, his words were a reminder to me of what God had done in Mike's life. Yes, Mike was a new man, had a changed life, a testimony to God's grace.[3]

I don't ever remember saying to God out loud, or even in prayer, that I expected our children to be problem-free or perfect. But somewhere in the deep recesses of my heart, I guess I did believe that the Lord would somehow put his stamp of approval on their lives. After all, as parents, we certainly were doing all the right things. Bill and I became Christians when our oldest sons were age two and four; a third son was born a year later. We worked at maintaining a Christian home, went to a Bible-believing church three times a week, and even enrolled our three sons in a Christian school. Surely God would bless our efforts and our family.

But as I stood in the driveway of our home on that June night in 1984, I didn't feel very blessed by God. My heart was hurting as never before. I screamed at God in anger. What had happened to the perfect plan? Where was God, anyhow? Our oldest son had graduated that afternoon from high school, and in a few short hours, had let us know he had no intention of following his parents' Christian lifestyle, or anything that resembled it.

That night would be the first of many nights, as Bill and I watched Mike being sucked into all the garbage the world had to offer. He seemed so angry and unhappy as he plummeted from one bad experience to another. It was a very painful time for our whole family.

A low point came when we had to ask Mike to move out of our home, as we could no longer tolerate his choices for his life. This was a mutual decision, as Michael wasn't happy with our lifestyle, either. As we watched our son leave our home that night, we were filled with mixed feelings of grief and relief. It had been a long year. We still weren't sure we had made the right decision, but we had to think of our other two sons at home. Our pastor had told us that there were rules and laws in a Christian home. Rules could be changed, but laws couldn't be broken, and Michael had certainly crossed the line.

So we released our son to his choices, knowing it was a downward track for him. We had exhausted all our human efforts as parents, and now we had to put feet on something we had given lip service to for the past twenty years—trusting God with our son. We knew in our hearts that God knew far better than we the plan for Mike's life.

We didn't see much of Mike after that. Occasionally he would come by for Sunday dinner, always looking worse than the time before. It was evident that things were falling apart in his life. We continued to watch and pray.

During this time the Lord began to work in our lives as parents. He taught us the power of prayer. He impressed upon us that we should share our burden with as many praying people as possible. Consequently, Mike was on prayer lists all over the country, from Texas to Wisconsin to California. Our own church held our whole family up in prayer. I vividly remember an Ash Wednesday service when we were to place prayer requests on the altar, and others would come and pray for that request. We joined a growth group that carried us through the roughest times in prayer.

It was also during this time that the Lord began to reveal to us, in a loving way through his Spirit, the faults of some of our parenting. This was a painful time, because our hearts meant well, but our doctrine had been harsh, thus creating a home full of legalistic do's and don'ts. We recognized ourselves as having problems similar to the Pharisees. We had to go before the Father with repentant hearts and ask him to cover our blunders with our children.

He also taught us about unconditional love, about unrealistic expectations, and acceptance and forgiveness. All these attributes we had received from the Father, we had failed to parent to our children, and especially to our firstborn son. Those were months of healing, as we received from our Lord his shower of grace. We continued to pray for Mike.

One afternoon in early May, Mike came through the back door of our home and sat down at the bar in the kitchen. We talked for a very few minutes. He looked tired, even old for his twenty years. It was obvious that life was beating away at him.

"Mom," he began, "I need you to pray for me."

"We've been praying, son," I replied. Mike began to cry.

The story was sad, all the things that can happen in a life running from God. He was broken in spirit. The tears were the first since he had been about ten years old—a long time coming. We did pray that day for God to work for good in Mike's life. Sometimes it's hard to know specifically what to ask God for. This was one of those times.

Mike left that day, and we were encouraged—no, we were thankful. God was moving. We began to see Mike more after that. He would drop by for dinner or just to visit. The problems were still there, but his heart was beginning to change, and so were ours. He asked if he could move back into our home. We weren't sure. We were scared, but eventually we worked out a sort of verbal contract with our son, and Mike came home.

We knew it would be a long road back. Healing needed to take place, and that would take time. It would take a lot of work, long talks, apologies, tears, laughter, and continued trust in God.

Our prayers changed for Mike at that point. He no longer needed our constant prayers for protection; he needed to walk his own walk with the Father. Most of all, he needed to know God's love, acceptance, and forgiveness, so that's how we prayed. It was a wonderful time—to trust God once again.

Mike struggled with many issues during that healing time. He had been drained of his self-esteem and motivation. He needed to recognize his potential and value as belonging to God. He began to attend church again, and found love and support here at Ginghamsburg Church. But most of all, he found the Father, who had been waiting all the time.

Finally, the time came when Mike became interested in his future. He began to look at various colleges and chose Taylor University, entering as a freshman in the fall of 1988. He took with him his life verse, Jeremiah 29:11: "For I know the plans I have for you," declares the LORD, "plans to prosper you and not to harm you, plans to give you hope and a future" (NIV).

Becoming a student took some adjustment for Mike. Concentration came hard and, being older than most freshmen, he felt uncomfortable. When he was given the opportunity to be a hall advisor in his dorm, he discovered that he had many gifts for dealing with people. He was respected and admired by his peers. During that time, it was a blessing to watch Mike develop into the person God was making him.

In May of 1992, Michael graduated from Taylor with a

double major in psychology and business. The graduation was wonderful, and as the class marched across the field, we quickly found our son in the crowd. Jeremiah 29:11 was taped on top of his graduation cap. We cried happy, thankful tears.

Michael is now working as a county probation officer and is looking at several graduate programs for the near future. He is living at home for the time being, and we are enjoying the years the locust had eaten, as God restores our relationship.

We are sharing Michael's story for several reasons. First, it is to encourage you who are struggling to know that God cares and answers prayer. He still performs miracles; claim his plan for you, as Jeremiah 29 promises. Second, it is to give glory and honor to Jesus Christ, the only One who gives new life.

Social Impact

Renewal is personal, but it also spills out on social institutions. Every great awakening has had a resulting major effect on the moral, economic, political, and cultural foundations of society itself. Historian William G. McLoughlin goes so far as to say that the great awakenings in American history have influenced most of our nation's social reforms. He contends that they are "the catalysts of social change."[4]

As the church becomes spiritually renewed, it moves against evil forces that oppress the people. It was a renewed church with a transformed people that fought slavery and illiteracy, and sent armies of missionaries around the world to teach, preach, and heal. Wesleyan renewal brought a moral and spiritual strength that averted a potential civil war in England and created many just changes in a corrupt neo-Industrial age. The church was at the heart of the struggle against racism in the 1960s, and a renewed church is needed today to carry on the continuing battle against the demonic forces of ethnic and cultural phobias that are raising their ugly heads across the globe.

A ministry that is holistic, that sees people as physical and spiritual beings with both physical and spiritual needs, must occur if there truly is to be a renewal of the Spirit of God. Transformation will occur in the lives of the people. The justice of God will be seen in the community of the transformed. As a result of the revival on the day of Pentecost, the believers sold their possessions and shared with others as they had need (Acts 2:45). This spirit of love can be manifested only by a work of the Spirit of God—not by gimmicks and human enthusiasm.

Do Numbers Count?

Numerical growth also is an important consideration in the renewal of the life of the church. Luke, the author of the book of Acts, was very concerned with the numerical growth of the church. He kept an ongoing record:

> So those who welcomed his message were baptized, and that day about three thousand persons were added. . . . And day by day the Lord added to their number those who were being saved. (Acts 2:41, 47b)
>
> But many of those who heard the word believed; and they numbered about five thousand. (Acts 4:4)
>
> Yet more than ever believers were added to the Lord, great numbers of both men and women. (Acts 5:14)

Numbers are important because each number represents an individual life. When individuals realize their infinite worth in the eyes of God and are transformed through faith in Jesus Christ, they become willfully committed to being part of God's awakening in the church and the world.

This book is an attempt to remind the church of first principles—a call to return to the First Love.

CHAPTER 1

THE LORDSHIP PRINCIPLE

Renewal happens as the church moves from a vague theism to clear faith in Jesus Christ.
• Telling about Jesus—the unique business of the church.
• It costs "everything" to follow Jesus.

For several mainline Protestant denominations this broadening of the belief system has reached the point that "inclusive" or "pluralistic" has replaced that original doctrinal statement as a rallying cry. Thus the original reason for the existence of that denomination has been eroded. . . .

The most difficult charge before the mainline Protestant denomination seeking to carve out a long-term and more productive future will be to define and project an identifiable theological position.[1]

Lyle E. Schaller

Who Do You Say That I Am?

Jesus put forth a critical question to his disciples: "Who do you say that I am?" (Matt. 16:15). This is the ultimate question of Christianity, for the identity of Jesus of Nazareth is Christianity.

And that question has become a disturbing and unclear question for much of the church today. A feature article, "The

Incredible Shrinking Jesus," which appeared in *Time* magazine (Jan. 1994), reported the findings of 74 biblical scholars (The Jesus Seminar) who had been meeting together twice a year, for the purpose of determining which sayings attributed to Jesus in the Gospels they considered to be authentic. The group determined that 82 percent of Jesus' words are not authentic. The results of their findings:

Jesus never claimed to be Messiah.

Jesus never delivered the Sermon on the Mount.

Jesus never cured any diseases.

Jesus never performed any miracles.

Jesus never was resurrected from the grave.

What happened to the body, then? The response of the committee—"Most likely it was consumed by wild dogs."

"Who do you say that I am?" The question demands an answer. Who is Jesus Christ? Is he truth for only some people, or is he truth for all people? Is he the Savior just for the church, or is he the Savior for the whole world? Is he private truth for some people, or public truth for all? This is the most critical question facing the church today, as it relates to our future. As Jurgen Moltmann has said, "The premise of Christology is Christian faith."[2]

The Object of Faith

The first and most important theological element that I was able to identify in the growth of Ginghamsburg Church was the clear focus on the person, work, and authority of Jesus Christ. He is the reason behind every action we take. "For 'In him we live and move and have our being'" (Acts 17:28).

The earliest Christian creed was simply "Jesus is Lord!" This early Jewish sect was considered rigid and unbending in its absorption with Jesus Christ and insistence on his uniqueness in God's plan of salvation. From Matthew to Revelation, we find a clear witness to Jesus' identity as God's unique Son and his absolute authority as the governing Lord of the universe. For example:

> Therefore let the entire house of Israel know with certainty that God has made him both Lord and Messiah, this Jesus whom you crucified. (Acts 2:36)

> There is salvation in no one else, for there is no other name under heaven given among mortals by which we must be saved. (Acts 4:12)

The author of the Gospel of John confirms the witness of the early Christian community concerning the uniqueness of Jesus:

> I am the way, and the truth, and the life. No one comes to the Father except through me. (John 14:6)

> Whoever has seen me has seen the Father. How can you say, "Show us the Father"? Do you not believe that I am in the Father and the Father is in me? (John 14:9b-10)

> I am the resurrection and the life. Those who believe in me, even though they die, will live, and everyone who lives and believes in me will never die. Do you believe this? (John 11:25)

For the New Testament church, Jesus was clearly more than a good moral teacher who pointed to God. He was the object of faith.

A Vague Theism

The church has a tendency to lose this clear focus on the person of Jesus Christ and to retreat into a vague theism. This can be seen in much of the theology of the 1960s: "God is love . . . love is God." For many of us, Jesus was just a guy holding sheep in a stained-glass window.

The message and focus of the New Testament church was not a vague concept of a benevolent God. It was a message of radical faith in the person of Jesus Christ. Again and again, we read, "They preached Jesus and the resurrection." From the first chapter of Acts to the last, we find a clear, focused witness of salvation in Jesus Christ, authenticated by the resurrection.

This point cannot be overemphasized. Jesus was not the example of truth. He was the *cause* of truth. Every act of the New Testament church was attributed to Jesus. Peter, in explaining the healing of a beggar who could not walk, proclaimed:

> Let it be known to all of you, and to all the people of Israel, that this man is standing before you in good health by the name of Jesus Christ of Nazareth, whom you crucified, whom God raised from the dead. This Jesus is
> "the stone that was rejected by you, the builders;
> it has become the cornerstone." (Acts 4:10-11)

The Jewish authorities considered this teaching about Jesus blasphemy against God. They were "much annoyed because they were teaching the people and proclaiming that in Jesus there is the resurrection of the dead." . . . "So they called them and ordered them not to speak or teach at all in the name of Jesus" (Acts 4:2, 18).

It is important to understand this total preoccupation with the person of Jesus of Nazareth. For the primitive church, there was no identity in God or salvation apart from him.

> Everyone who believes that Jesus is the Christ has been born of God, and everyone who loves the parent loves the child. . . . Who is it that conquers the world but the one who believes that Jesus is the Son of God? (1 John 5:1, 5)

> Those who believe in the Son of God have the testimony in their hearts. Those who do not believe in God have made him a liar by not believing in the testimony that God has given

concerning his Son. And this is the testimony: God gave us eternal life, and this life is in his Son. Whoever has the Son has life; whoever does not have the Son of God does not have life.
(1 John 5:10-12)

Why did the New Testament church make such bold sweeping assertions? Those people were thoroughly convinced that this carpenter from Nazareth had literally been resurrected from the grave. God had confirmed the uniqueness of Jesus by that great historical event. To the believers in the early church, the resurrection was not a symbolic faith statement, but a supernatural intervention of God in space and time. Paul confirms this literal interpretation:

Christ died for our sins in accordance with the scriptures, and that he was buried, and that he was raised on the third day in accordance with the scriptures, and that he appeared to Cephas, then to the twelve. Then he appeared to more than five hundred brothers and sisters at one time, most of whom are still alive, though some have died. Then he appeared to James, then to all the apostles. Last of all, as to one untimely born, he appeared also to me. (1 Cor. 15:3*b*-8)

Paul is listing eyewitnesses. He is documenting and validating the accuracy of this event. That is why he places such an emphasis on the appearance to five hundred witnesses "at one time" and emphasizes that "most are still alive." Paul is saying, "If you don't believe me, go and check it out for yourselves, with the many others who witnessed this great event." He goes on:

If Christ has not been raised, then our proclamation has been in vain and your faith has been in vain. . . . If Christ has not been raised, your faith is futile and you are still in your sins. Then those also who have died in Christ have perished. If for this life only we have hoped in Christ, we are of all people most to be pitied. (1 Cor. 15:14, 17-19)

Paul is boldly asserting, "If the body of Jesus is lying lifeless and molding in some grave, then our faith is worthless. He is not who he said he was, and we are the greatest fools of all. So let's all go home and quit playing church. Let's stop lying to people by telling them that God did something he really didn't do."

It is very important to recognize Paul's concern for the credibility of his unwavering acceptance of the resurrection and the integrity of his testimony. In First Corinthians 15:15, Paul gives a clear statement to the intent of total honesty in his witness when he says, in effect, "If we said Christ resurrected from the grave, and he didn't, not only would we be liars, but we would be lying against God, because we said that God has done something that God has not done."

The New Testament church believed in a literal resurrection, not a symbolic resurrection. For this reason, they had a clear conviction that Jesus Christ was different from any other person who ever lived. No one had ever said or done the things that Jesus did. The early Christians were so convinced of the validity of the witness concerning Jesus and the fact of the resurrection that they were willing to lay down their lives for this man. Those people were willing to forsake everything they knew. They were shunned, persecuted, considered a cult, thrown out of the temple, and imprisoned—not for a vague theism, but because they believed that Jesus Christ was the living Lord, the object of their faith.

Renewal—Returning to the First Love

I know your works, your toil and your patient endurance. I know that you cannot tolerate evildoers; you have tested those who claim to be apostles but are not, and have found them to be false. I also know that you are enduring patiently and bearing up for the sake of my name, and that you have not grown weary. But I have this against you, that you have abandoned the love you had at first. Remember then from what you have fallen; repent, and do the works you did at first. (Rev. 2:2-5)

The church's first major struggle after the early persecutions was the rise of great heresies, considered heresies because of their interpretation of the most fundamental Christian doctrine—the person of Christ. Arianism, one of the most widely held heresies, was rejected at the Council of Nicaea in 325, and again at the Council at Constantinople in 381, because it blatantly denied the full divinity of Christ.

The growing popularity of heresies forced the church to develop a formal body of teaching on the person and work of Christ. One of the early writers of this theology, who insisted upon the deity of Jesus, was Augustine of Hippo (354–430), considered one of the greatest theologians of the early church. The Protestant and Catholic Reformers were greatly influenced by his work, even more than a thousand years later.

Augustine had a dramatic conversion experience at the age of thirty-three, after years of philosophical search and sensual living. He had struggled with the power of sin and the weakness of the human will, and could identify with Paul's statement, "For I do not do the good I want, but the evil I do not want is what I do" (Rom. 7:19).[3] After his conversion, Augustine saw Christ as more than a mere man or moral teacher, but "that He merited the highest authority." He believed that conversion necessitated putting "on the Lord Jesus Christ."[4]

Augustine clarified a biblical theology for the church which stressed human impotence without divine grace, justification by faith in Christ, as opposed to works, and Christ's sacrifice as being sufficient for salvation.[5] Augustine's clear Christ-centeredness spurred the renewal that occurred during both the Protestant Reformation and the Counter-Reformation in the Catholic Church during the sixteenth and seventeenth centuries.

Martin Luther, a priest and former Augustinian monk, objected to the medieval church system and its departure from

Paul's biblical teaching, which affirmed that salvation is found simply through faith in Jesus Christ. Luther emphasized that justification was not obtained by performing good works. He felt that the focus and authority of the church had shifted from the person of Christ to the institution. Luther equated this realization to a Damascus-Road experience.[6] Through his teachings, the church began to experience transformational renewal by rediscovering the First Love.

Renewal happens as the church moves from a vague theism to a clear faith in Jesus Christ. The focus of the church is not church, but Jesus! God is made known to us in Christ. Faith comes alive in Christ. Lives are transformed and empowered through Christ.

The same movement of the Spirit that affected the Reformers was also moving among those who were committed to staying in the Catholic Church. A clear focus on Christ as the focus of faith and worship was also at the heart of the Counter-Reformation. As A. G. Dickens writes, "And even after Luther's revolt, the highest Catholic achievements were those of men and women who believed themselves to be seeking Christ rather than fighting Luther."[7]

Ignatius Loyola (1491–1556) was to the Catholic Church and the Counter-Reformation what Luther was to the Protestant Reformation. Loyola had a conversion experience six years after Luther's, but he was committed to renewal within the Catholic Church. He founded the Society of Jesus (the Jesuits), with the express purpose of renewing the church and taking Christ to the unchurched people of the world. The Jesuits shared Christ with a missionary zeal. Dickens states:

> To their leadership Ignatius brought far more than a series of heroic gestures: the new society grouped itself not only round the man but round a scheme of devotion clearly embodied in his "Spiritual Exercises" . . . the devotional method and idiom remained intensely Christocentric.[8]

Ignatius Loyola was calling people back to following Christ in a radical way. The Jesuits and their focus on Christ became the primary vehicle, both for carrying renewal throughout the church and for reaching the unchurched.

Teresa of Avila (1515–1582), from whom Mother Teresa of Calcutta has taken her name, and St. John of the Cross (1542–1591) were Reformers who also played key roles in the renewal movement within the Catholic Church. Both had a consuming passion to experience Christ and make him known. They taught the church much about the necessity of personal time spent with Christ in prayer and meditation.

These Reformers clearly understood that apart from a personal, dynamic growing relationship with Christ, the church has no life. Christ is our life!

> I pray that out of his glorious riches he may strengthen you with power through his Spirit in your inner being, so that Christ may dwell in your hearts through faith. And I pray that you, being rooted and established in love, may have power, together with all the saints, to grasp how wide and long and high and deep is the love of Christ, and to know this love that surpasses knowledge—that you may be filled to the measure of all the fullness of God. (Eph. 3:16-19 NIV)

John Wesley (1703–1791) began ministering in the Anglican Church of England, a church that again had cooled in its passion for Jesus Christ. His ministry was marked by years of frustration and uncertainty before his conversion on May 24, 1738. He had even confessed to the Moravian leader Peter Bohler that he doubted his own salvation. Shortly after a disastrous missionary journey to Georgia, Wesley wrote concerning his ignorance about Christ as the object of faith:

> In my return to England, January 1738, being in imminent danger of death, and very uneasy on that account, I was strongly convinced that the cause of that uneasiness was unbelief; and that gaining a true, living faith was the "one thing needful" for

me. But still I fixed not this faith on its right object: I meant only faith in God, not faith in or through Christ. Again, I knew not that I was wholly void of this faith; but only thought I had not enough of it. So that when Peter Bohler, whom God prepared for me as soon as I came to London, affirmed of true faith in Christ (which is but one) that it had those two fruits inseparably attending it, "dominion over sin and constant peace from a sense of forgiveness," I was quite amazed, and looked upon it as a new gospel. If this was so, it was clear I had not faith. . . . And accordingly the next day he came again with three others, all of whom testified, of their own personal experience, that a true living faith in Christ is inseparable from a sense of pardon for all past and freedom from all present sins.[9]

In the week that followed, Wesley shifted his focus from a vague benevolent God to the living Christ.

In the evening I went very unwillingly to a society in Aldersgate Street, where one was reading Luther's preface to the Epistle to the Romans. About a quarter before nine, while he was describing the change which God works in the heart through faith in Christ, I felt my heart strangely warmed. I felt I did trust in Christ, Christ alone for salvation; and an assurance was given me that He had taken away my sins, even mine, and saved me from the law of sin and death.[10]

Wesley wrote this journal entry the following day: "The moment I awaked, 'Jesus, Master,' was in my heart and in my mouth; and I found all my strength lay in keeping my eye fixed upon Him, and my soul waiting on Him continually."[11]

Wesley was quickly branded an enthusiast by the church for his zealous insistence upon conversion through personal faith in Jesus Christ. Pulpit after pulpit was closed to him because he called the people to repent of their dead institutionalism and return to their first love in Jesus Christ. John Wesley rigidly believed and taught that there is no salvation apart from the atoning work of Jesus Christ. According to Burtner and Chiles,

[Wesley] declares that turning from the atonement is equivalent to embracing deism or paganism; he regards either defection as disastrous to the life of faith. . . . A letter to William Law on this subject shows Wesley to have been accusing, even bitter, because he failed to find in Law's writings the gospel pronouncement of Christ's atoning work for man. Faith in this atoning work is for Wesley the sole way to salvation.[12]

The church has once again lost its clear focus on the person of Jesus Christ and his unique exclusive role in God's redemptive plan. But a new wind is blowing. New voices are being heard in the church. These voices are reminding us that "*in Christ* God was reconciling the world to himself" (2 Cor. 5:19). The foundation principle of renewal—in Christ!

I want to add a word of caution. Renewal is much more than adding a little more Jesus to the mix. A little more Jesus won't work. Jesus must be the absolute focus. It must be an all or nothing proposition. The key for renewal is a clear focus on Jesus Christ as the object of faith and the cause of truth. In a post-Christian age, clarity of focus is now more necessary than ever.

Absolute Authority

In my denomination, when people enter into the covenant of membership with a local church, they are asked this crucial question: Do you confess Jesus Christ as your Lord and Savior and pledge your allegiance to his kingdom?

My family and I had the privilege of traveling and preaching in Germany during the summer of 1990. We were invited by a group of informal churches called Gemeindes, born out of the Jesus movement during the 1960s and 1970s. These informal churches meet in rented buildings, beer gardens, YMCAs, and traditional church facilities at untraditional times. While the state church (Lutheran) has an older, more rural population, the membership of the Gemeindes is very young, almost exclusively under forty. Most are twenty-something.

While the Gemeindes are "unofficial," they offer an exciting approach to reaching unchurched people in a mainly unchurched culture. The Gemeindes tend to average between 30 and 200 in their meetings. Though many are university students, a great number are being drawn from the punk culture, and even some of the "skin heads" are being transformed. Needless to say, these informal congregations make for an interesting mix.

We had been in Germany for about two weeks, and I was speaking on a Sunday evening to the congregation of *Rhema Gemeinde*. They were using the facilities of a Lutheran church in Darmstadt. The German language does not have a separate word for *Lord*. To translate the word *Lord*, Germans use the word *Herr*. *Herr* can mean Lord, master, and several other authoritative titles, such as judge; it is also used to refer to a man as Mister.

I was openly sharing my frustration of having to refer to Jesus as "Mister Jesus" instead of "Lord Jesus," and commented that the word was totally inadequate in expressing Jesus' true identity. A young man, a master's student in engineering at a local university, stood up in the back of the church and called out, right in the middle of my discourse, "We may not have a separate and distinct word for Lord, but you Americans might as well not have. You have forgotten what it means."

He was right. His response was prophetic. Many of us in the western church today have lost sight of what the word *Lord* means. For many, it is just a title, like Reverend or Doctor or Sir. So when we say "Lord Jesus," we really mean no more than Mr. Jesus.

In the New Testament church, the meaning was clear. "Lord" meant the one who had absolute authority. Caesar was the only person who could be called Lord with a capital "L." The typical greeting on the street in the Roman empire would include the affirmation, "Caesar is Lord." And the response would echo this affirmation: "Yes, Caesar is truly Lord." It was the law. To fail to publicly acknowledge Caesar's claim to deity and absolute authority could mean arrest and ultimately death.

The word also means *owner.* A slave would refer to his or her owner as "lord" with a small "l." This meant that the slave was bound to the authority of the master and had no rights of his or her own. The only possible response was one of complete obedience.

Many Americans have difficulty with the concept of obedience. We are used to a democracy that gives us many different choices and opportunities for input and involvement. We can choose where to live, what to do for a vocation, who to marry, and the organizations we will join. We even choose what we want to believe or not believe. We can be Republican, Democrat, Socialist, or even Communist. At the heart of a democracy lies the concept of freedom of choice. Jesus, however, did not come proclaiming a democracy. He came proclaiming a kingdom.

There is a major difference between a kingdom and a democracy. In a democracy, the people determine the rules of the game. They set up a charter or a constitution and participate in the running of the organization. Each person accepts a responsibility, and there are dues and money-making projects to support the purpose. Each person has a vote or a say in the operation of the organization.

In a kingdom, all rules are determined by the king. Each person is given a responsibility. Kings do not have dues or money-making projects—they set tariffs. They do not need to ask for my consent—they command! The biggest difference between a democracy and a kingdom lies in the concept of choice. In a democracy, choice lies in the hands of the governed. In a kingdom, choice lies solely with the king.

Many people today treat the church as if it were a democracy; the same rules that apply to the Girl Scouts and the Kiwanis apply to the church. It is often difficult to tell the difference between the church and many service clubs. We like to think of ourselves as "volunteers," who pick and choose what we will do for God and God's church. We even minimize the importance of the work when we go through the annual nomination process, asking people to "help out" in noncostly ways:

"You wouldn't want to help us out by serving on the education committee this year, would you?"

"Well, I don't know. What's involved?"

"Oh, not much, not much at all—you only have to attend one meeting a month."

Here at Ginghamsburg, we are realizing that it costs everything to follow Jesus. If we ask someone to carry out the trash, and he or she asks what's involved, we now respond by saying, "everything!"

The early church understood clearly the meaning of the affirmation "Jesus is Lord!" When a Christian was greeted on the street with "Caesar is Lord" the response often caused much controversy. Christians recognized only one absolute authority and owner: "Jesus is Lord!" The Roman colosseum did a tremendous business because of the Christians' stubborn insistence concerning Jesus' absolute authority.

Volunteer or Slave?

Who among you would say to your slave who has just come in from plowing or tending sheep in the field, "Come here at once and take your place at the table"? Would you not rather say to him, "Prepare supper for me, put on your apron and serve me while I eat and drink; later you may eat and drink"? Do you thank the slave for doing what was commanded? So you also, when you have done all that you were ordered to do, say, "We are worthless slaves; we have done only what we ought to have done!" (Luke 17:7-10)

Jesus quickly gets to the heart of the "volunteer" mentality of service in this passage. The word for "servant" is *bondslave*. A bondslave, or servant, did not work for wages, but lived under the authority and ownership of a master. The servant's ear was pierced, and an earring with the emblem of the owner was placed in the ear. The earring meant that the slave was bound to that household for life.

Slaves had no rights or privileges. Individual identity was exchanged for the identity of the masters. The initials on the earrings became their own. Slaves had nothing that was personal. Everything belonged to the masters, even the clothes they had on their backs. There was no distinction between work time and personal time for slaves. Every moment belonged to the masters. That is the key point that Jesus is making in this parable.

Slaves in middle-eastern culture rarely lived to see the age of thirty. They were expected to be in the fields from first light to last light, from six in the morning until about nine at night. On the way to and from the fields, they milked and fed the livestock.

When a slave came in after a grueling schedule, the master did not say, "Oh, you poor slave. You have been working so hard all day. Why don't you take a quick shower and then come on over here and sit down in my recliner, and I will get you the newspaper and a cool drink."

Instead, the master would say, "Slave, look at you—you are a mess. Hurry and get cleaned up and come back and get our drink orders and fix our supper."

Dinner in that culture was the highlight of the day. Without television or any of the other distractions that invade our family time, people actually stayed around the family table and talked during most of the evening. They would lie prone around the table, on pillows.

The supper meal was one of the most intimate parts of the day. It is the word Jesus uses when he says, "Listen! I am standing at the door, knocking; if you hear my voice and open the door, I will come in to you and eat with you, and you with me" (Rev. 3:20). The word translated "eat" in this passage literally means "supper meal," the intimate meal that was the highlight of the day.

Needless to say, much preparation went into this meal. But guess who was responsible for preparing it? Right! You guessed it—the good old bondservant. After a full day in the field and tending the animals, the slave had to come in, clean up, and prepare a major dinner. And often this also involved the over-sight of entertainment. Only after the drinks were served, the food was on the table, the belly dancers had finished, and the master was put to bed, could the slaves finally help themselves to any of the leftover food before falling exhausted into bed.

Jesus said that we must identify with those slaves if we are truly to be his followers. We must come to that point when we realize, "We are unworthy servants; we have only done our duty." Volunteer is the language of the club. Slave is the language of the kingdom of God.

God's Choice—Not Mine

As the people of Jesus, we need to reach the place where we understand that the call of God always comes in the form of a command. Nowhere in Scripture do we hear God asking whether anyone would like to "help out."

In the third chapter of Exodus, we find Moses working in his father-in-law's business. While on a business trip, he had a personal encounter with God, in which God tells him to go to Egypt and appear before Pharaoh. He is to tell Pharaoh that God has not been blind to the whole issue of oppression and that God expects Pharaoh to right the wrong by letting the Israelites go.

Moses, at this point, does not understand that the call of God upon his life is not a multiple-choice option. He proceeds to list reasons why it would be better for God to choose someone else: "Lord, I can't do that. . . . I've never been to seminary. I . . . I'm not a very eloquent speaker. I even stutter. Pharaoh would never believe me. I don't have any credentials. . . . Have you considered my brother Aaron? He is more polished than I am. . . . Please send someone else—anyone else!" Moses spends almost two chapters trying to talk his way out of the inevitable. Finally, after God has patiently listened to these excuses, he reminds Moses that obedience is not an option.

A king does not ask for consent—he decrees. Jesus reminded his followers of this great truth when he said, "You did not choose me but I chose you. And I appointed you to go and bear fruit, fruit that will last" (John 15:16). We do not vote for Jesus, or even choose Jesus. He is the absolute authority—the owner—the one who calls us and sends us. Our only response can be one of obedience. When we recognize the authority of Jesus Christ, we realize that the ordering of our daily activities is God's choice—not our own.

Good Excuses

As they were going along the road, someone said to him, "I will follow you wherever you go." And Jesus said to him, "Foxes have holes, and birds of the air have nests; but the Son of Man has nowhere to lay his head." To another he said, "Follow me." But he said, "Lord, first let me go and bury my father." But Jesus said to him, "Let the dead bury their own dead; but as for you, go and proclaim the kingdom of God." Another said, "I will follow you, Lord; but let me first say farewell to those at my home." Jesus said to him, "No one who puts a hand to the plow and looks back is fit for the kingdom of God." (Luke 9:57-62)

A pastor I knew had the opportunity to meet Mother Teresa while he was traveling in India. On a whim, he decided to visit the Missionaries of Charity headquarters while he was staying in Calcutta. He wasn't even sure whether Mother Teresa was in the country, but it was worth the chance.

After an adventurous cab trip through crowded streets, he arrived at the simple structure that houses one of the greatest testimonies to the reality of the resurrection in the world. He knocked at the door, and a young novice in the simple white and blue sari of the Missionaries of Charity answered. She listened as he explained the intent of his mission. By the good graces of God, Mother Teresa was in the country. And even better, she was working in the headquarters that day.

The young disciple ushered him into a simple parlor, and after a brief wait, the pastor could hardly believe his eyes. There she stood! A little frail, bent-over woman, overflowing with the presence of Jesus. She graciously spent about twenty minutes with the young clergyman. Then, not wishing to intrude on any more of her time, he stood up to express his appreciation and depart, but before he left, he asked, "What advice might you have to offer a young preacher?"

"Only this," she said. "Preach Jesus, the true Jesus, the real Jesus, the resurrected Jesus, and not a Jesus of people's imaginations."

I often get the feeling that people are following a Jesus of their imagination and not the real Jesus, the risen Lord of the universe. And nowhere is this more apparent than in this passage of Scripture. A man comes up to Jesus and makes a bold declaration of allegiance: "I will follow you wherever you go!" Jesus responds by showing this person the concrete reality of what this obedience will entail: "Even the foxes have dens and the birds nests, but the Son of Man is committed to an itinerant lifestyle. Can you really make that kind of commitment?"

My wife and I could hardly wait to receive our first full-time appointment after seminary. We went to meet the Pastor Parish Committee with great anticipation. The interview went well, as each of us had a chance to share our dreams and visions for ministry. There was a real inner affirmation that God's hand was in this appointment. The committee told us that they would be renting an apartment for us, but until that time, we would be living with an elderly widower in the church. For the next six weeks we lived in an upstairs attic, with a squeaky bed, a picnic table, and a rocking chair.

I remember lying in bed the Saturday night before the first Sunday in my new appointment, thinking about these words of Jesus: "The Son of Man has an itinerant lifestyle—follow me!"

What a privilege we have in being able to participate in this great adventure. A word of caution: This itinerant lifestyle is not only for pastors. This challenge is for all who call Jesus Lord!

Jesus commands another man to follow him. This person, like Moses, confuses a decree with a suggestion, and he really comes up with a good excuse. I have been a pastor for more than twenty years, and I have heard a lot of excuses, but his is the best: "Lord, first let me go and bury my father." He even uses the title "Lord" in referring to Jesus, but obviously, he does not understand the magnitude of its meaning.

Jesus is quick, almost coldly cruel in elevating this man's understanding: "Let the dead bury their own dead, but you go and proclaim the kingdom of God." Jesus is the absolute authority. There is no excuse for anything other than absolute obedience.

Many of us have a warehouse full of reasons why we are less than what Christ calls us to be. We often say that Jesus is first in our lives, but in reality, he comes after careers, relationships, clubs, golf outings, band practice, football, baseball, soccer, and even yard work. That is why I am convinced that most people in the church today are following a Jesus of their imagination, not the risen Lord of the universe.

Then another man wants to follow, but with a condition: "First let me go back and say good-bye to my family." But we cannot follow Jesus with any conditional clauses attached. "No one who puts a hand to the plow and looks back is fit for the kingdom of God" (Luke 9:62).

In our denomination's tradition, the membership vow is powerful: "Do you accept Jesus Christ as your Lord and Savior and do you pledge your allegiance to his kingdom?" The conviction that Jesus is Lord has been the key theological factor of every awakening. God is a vague philosophical idea until I meet God face-to-face in the person of Jesus Christ. Jesus does not allow me to create a god in my own image who serves me and my particular prejudices.

As I face Jesus and understand his authority, I must deal with my own self-absorption. Like Zacchaeus the tax collector, I realize that I have a great responsibility to others if I enter a relationship with Jesus (Luke 19:1-9). Like the woman caught in adultery, I hear Jesus' words about a full pardon and the necessity of moral living (John 8:1-11). Following Jesus involves everything. He is not just one part of life—he *is* life! "Do you pledge your allegiance to his kingdom?" This means that your allegiance to Jesus Christ and his kingdom must supersede any and all other allegiances in your life.

I have two friends who took this vow very seriously. Tom and Elaine Sampley discovered a personal relationship with Christ and became very active in ministry at Ginghamsburg while we were still a very small church. Like most baby boomers, they were focused on raising their children and fulfilling their material and relational needs. I first met Tom and Elaine in the lean years. Tom was working two jobs, while trying to establish a fledgling real estate business. Long hours and tight finances made for the typical home tensions. After several years of hard work, Tom and Elaine began to experience financial success, and they built their dream home, complete with swimming pool, in a prestigious neighborhood.

They had lived in their new home less than a year when Tom shared a new sense of calling with a small group of men who met together every Thursday morning: "Would you guys pray for me? I really don't understand what is going on. But I believe God wants me to go into full-time ministry."

We prayed and we listened. Tom and Elaine sold their business and their dream home, and, at age forty-five, set off for Bible school. They spent the next two years exhausting their resources on tuition, living expenses, and the tuition of their two older children, still in college. Today Tom is the admissions director of The Word of Life Bible Center in Schroon Lake, New York. Remember:

We do not live to ourselves, and we do not die to ourselves. If we live, we live to the Lord, and if we die, we die to the Lord; so then, whether we live or whether we die, we are the Lord's. For to this end Christ died and lived again, so that he might be Lord of both the dead and the living. (Rom. 14:7-9)

The Good New About Jesus

Philip was traveling the desert road south from Jerusalem to Gaza. On the way, he met an Ethiopian eunuch who was on official business for the queen. The Ethiopian had been reading from the book of Isaiah. Philip took advantage of the situation and, beginning at the passage from which the Ethiopian had been reading, "proclaimed to him the good news about Jesus" (Acts 8:35*b*).

Telling the good news about Jesus is the unique business of the church. The YMCA has excellent camping and recreation programs. There are many effective social-service agencies in our communities. Multitudes of clubs and organizations welcome our people's participation and involvement. We can offer those around us only one thing that these organizations do not already offer—JESUS CHRIST. We must be careful not to water down the message with a vague theism.

Jesus Christ said, "And I, when I am lifted up from the earth, will draw all people to myself" (John 12:32). In my preaching, teaching, counseling, and administration at Ginghamsburg, I have sought to do this one thing—lift up Jesus Christ. Renewal theology, reduced to the least complicated denominator, is simply lifting up Jesus in every act of the church. When Jesus becomes the focus of the life of the local church, new life comes to dry bones, and people begin to stand up and become a vital army.

Chapter 11

THE BIBLICAL PRINCIPLE

> Scriptural truth is the primary source for what we believe and do.
> - Biblical preaching, speaking with the authority of the Word of God
> - For transformation, not information only

When the king heard the words of the book of the law, he tore his clothes. Then the king commanded the priest Hilkiah Ahikam son of Shaphan, Achbor son of Micaiah, Shaphan the secretary, and the king's servant Asaiah, saying, "Go, inquire of the LORD for me, for the people, and for all Judah, concerning the words of this book that has been found; for great is the wrath of the LORD that is kindled against us, because our ancestors did not obey the words of this book, to do according to all that is written concerning us."

2 Kings 22:11-13

Getting Back to the Book

Josiah was born during the last half of the seventh century B.C., during the reign of the corrupt king Manasseh. It was probably the lowest, darkest moment in Israel's history. For years, the people had been assimilating the pagan practices of the surrounding cultures and disregarding God's command to remain separate and distinct. Preceding kings of Judah had even accepted the practice of sun worship.

Manasseh surpassed them all. He imported pagan priests and established male cult prostitutes throughout the countryside. Pagan deities and images were erected in the temple. Offerings were made to Baal and to the female fertility goddess, Asherah. Human sacrifices were being made in the Hinnom Valley, to the pagan god Molech. Manasseh even sank to the despicable act of sacrificing his own son in the fire (2 Kings 21). The people were turning to mediums and spiritualists for guidance. Household gods and idols flourished. God's people were adrift in a sea of spiritual and moral confusion. The clear call of the God of Abraham, Isaac, and Jacob was no longer heard.

But a voice of reformation cried out from the ashes. Josiah, who became the boy king of Judah at the age of eight, would be God's agent for renewal.

> He did what was right in the sight of the LORD, and walked in the ways of his ancestor David; he did not turn aside to the right or to the left. For in the eighth year of his reign, while he was still a boy, he began to seek the God of his ancestor David. (2 Chron. 34:2-3)

During the early years of his reign, Josiah began a series of sweeping reforms. He tore down the regional altars of sacrifice and attempted to restore the temple as the central place of worship. He worked at purging the pagan influences that had been assimilated into the faith. The altars of the Baals, Asherah poles, idols and images, were smashed to pieces. The corrupt priests were removed.

When he was twenty-six, Josiah turned his attention to the repair and reform of the temple in Jerusalem. A crucial discovery was made during these repairs, a discovery that has been essential to every renewal of God's people. While the workers were restoring the temple, a dusty old misplaced book was found by Hilkiah, the high priest. It was the Book of the Law of the Lord that had been given through Moses. Its vital message had gone unheard by the people for decades. The Mosaic Book of the Law was brought to King Josiah. When he heard the words of the book, he realized that Judah had drastically deviated from God's plan. They had been a people building without a blueprint. Josiah had the people gather at the temple to hear the words of the book that had been found on a dusty shelf. The result was radical revitalization! The people turned from dead institutionalism to the living God.

The Standard for Faith

Renewal grows out of rediscovery of biblical truth. The church rediscovers the lost book and reaffirms the unique, timeless revelation from God through its transforming message. The Bible becomes the standard for faith in the midst of a sea of voices crying to be heard in the philosophical and moral wilderness.

What happened to Judah has recurred throughout church history. Martin Luther discovered the lost book out of a sense of frustration with the tired, shifting traditions of the church. He experienced the voice of God through the book of Romans. His "Sola Scriptura" approach to the faith fanned the flames of the Reformation. Luther translated the Bible into the common language of the masses, which inspired both Protestant and Catholic reformations.

Nearly two hundred years later, John Wesley heard God's voice while attending a Moravian Bible-study group. They were studying Luther's notes on the book of Romans. Wesley's life, and the lives of millions of others influenced by his teachings, would never again be the same. He became "a man of one book." For Wesley, the Bible was the last word in determining the boundaries of the Christian faith.

> The Christian rule of right and wrong is the Word of God, the writings of the Old and New Testament; all that the prophets and "holy men of old" wrote "as they were moved by the Holy

Ghost"; all that Scripture which was "given by inspiration of God," and which is indeed "profitable for doctrine," or teaching the whole will of God; "for reproof" of what is contrary thereto; for "correction" of error; and "for instruction," or training us up, "in righteousness." (2 Tim. 3:16)

This is a lantern unto a Christian's feet, and a light in all his paths. This alone he receives as his rule of right or wrong, of whatever is really good or evil.[1]

Wesley held Scripture above reason, experience, and tradition in determining Christian truth. He saw Scripture as the final testing ground of authenticity.

My ground is the Bible. Yea, I am a Bible-bigot. I follow it in all things, both great and small. . . .

In matters of religion I regard no writings but the inspired. Tauler, Behmen, and an whole army of Mystic authors are with me nothing to St. Paul. In every point I appeal "to the law and the testimony," and value no authority but this.[2]

Robert Chiles writes:

[Wesley] was well acquainted with and drew upon the early church fathers and the lessons of church history. He was particularly attentive to those factors that he believed had obscured and distorted the realities of primitive Christianity. He held that the great councils of the church were subject to error, and he insisted on checking their pronouncements against the Scriptures. In this, as in all things, Wesley contended that the written Word of God stand as the sole authority for Christians and the church.[3]

Beyond Opinions

Week after week, countless numbers of our people slumber through our sermons. Pastors often wonder why parishioners are critical or indifferent toward their preaching and bemoan sermons that last longer than fifteen or twenty minutes.

People are longing for a word from God. They are not interested in our personal opinions. They want more than the latest book review or political commentary. In an age of uncertainty and materialistic self-centeredness, our people yearn for a message from God. In a time when the nuclear family is being redefined through divorce and single parenting, does God still speak with a voice of hope? In an age of global political and economic instability, growing racial tension, uncertain moral boundaries, and AIDS—is there a word from God?

Have you ever wondered why so many people were willing to follow a nonconformist, an upstart preacher like John the Baptist, into the wilderness? John could have been accused of not having both oars in the water. He was eccentric. Not many people of his day wore animal skins or observed his dietary habits. He did not have the best pastoral attitude, calling people "brood of vipers" and the like.

Yet John preached to standing-room-only crowds in the desert, and there was no air conditioning! It was not for lack of religious leaders. Jerusalem was full of liberal and conservative teachers, well versed in their religious opinions and theological jargon. John did not even have formal theological training. But he spoke with a different kind of authority. He did not say "I think" or "I believe" or "I feel." John spoke with the authority of the Word of God.

Faith Comes from Hearing

Our people have become biblically illiterate. They are no longer "a people of one book." For many, the Bible is a filing system for sacred family treasures stored between its pages. It is hidden away on a shelf or ornamentally displayed on a table. In our Sunday school classes, we study books about the Book or hear stories from the Book, but we rarely study the Book itself. Our pastors have lost the art of relevant biblical preaching. Many see the Bible as a collection of nonrelated ancient books that are irrelevant to our highly complex technological society. They fail to see the amazing interrelatedness of these books that tell one story. It is the story of paradise lost and paradise regained. It is the message of God's far-reaching and never failing love. It is a history of personal victory and hope. It is the promise of purpose and direction through Jesus Christ.

My formative years fell during the 1960s, when many young people my age were looking for answers to very real problems. I grew up in a fairly typical mainstream church. It was neither hot nor cold. My family rarely missed worship or Sunday school. I remember studying the book *Catcher in the Rye* in my freshman Sunday school class, with a teacher who claimed to be agnostic. My church was offering no prophetic messages of hope or purpose.

Like many my age, I was greatly influenced by the British music invasion that came with the Beatles. My parents gave me my first guitar when I was in the eighth grade. By my junior year in high school, the band I played in managed its own teen club. My highest grade that year was a "D." I finished the year with two "Fs" and three "Ds." Things only got worse during my senior year. Two of the guys in the group were arrested for the possession of drugs. One of my teachers changed an "F" to a "D minus," less than a week before graduation, which allowed me to graduate with my class.

Out of a sense of desperation, I began to ask some pretty basic questions: "Is there a God?" "Is God good?" "What is God like?" "Does God care for me?" One night, either out of boredom or in a desperate search for purpose, I pulled out a dust-covered book from the stand next to my bed. It was the Bible I had been given in my third-grade Sunday school class. For some reason, I skipped over the Old Testament and went right to the Gospel stories. I probably would have quit prematurely, if I had started in Genesis or Leviticus.

As I began the nightly ritual of reading from this book, something strange began to happen in my life. I found a magnetic attraction to the person of Jesus. "Is this what God is like?" I asked myself. I could hardly believe the words of Jesus that I read in John 8, concerning the woman who was caught in adultery: "Neither do I condemn you."

Is it possible, I thought, that God's love and forgiveness is this broad? Could it be that God's goodness extends to those who are caught red-handed? And what is this? Jesus is the friend of sinners! He travels with undesirables. He invites prostitutes to be his friends. This is too good to be true! This means that there is hope for me.

There was something radically different about the man in these stories. He even got into hassles with religious people. (We do seem to be the source of many of the problems in the church.) I could not wait to read more about him each night. After all my years in the church, I was seeing the uniqueness of Jesus for the first time. It was not an overnight experience. I did not know any terminology, like "born again." But somehow I deeply sensed that life's purpose could be found in him. I knew that Christ, and Christ alone, held the key to what I was yearning for deep within my spirit.

Confrontation with the Word of God awakens faith. "So faith comes from what is heard, and what is heard comes through the word of Christ" (Rom. 10:17). As we are exposed to the words of this book, our spirit bears witness with God's Spirit to the reality of life found in Christ.

The Scripture does not bear witness to itself. It does not call us to believe in Scripture; it calls us to believe in the One whom God has sent.

> Now Jesus did many other signs in the presence of his disciples, which are not written in this book. But these are written so that you may come to believe that Jesus is the Messiah, the Son of God, and that through believing you may have life in his name. (John 20:30-31)

The Bible is the word of God with the small "w" that points us to the living Word of God with the capital "W." The focus is not the Bible; the focus is Christ! The Bible is not an end in itself, but a means to an end, which is life in Christ.

When the Ethiopian eunuch asked Philip to explain a passage of Scripture from Isaiah, Philip did not give him a long cerebral theological discourse. He didn't say: "Oh, I am glad you asked. Isaiah was really written by two different authors at two different points in history. So there is really a first and a second Isaiah. The author was probably symbolically refering to historical events of his time period, and not intentionally aware of the prophetic implications." The eunuch would have been either confused or asleep by the time Philip had finished the second sentence.

Philip did not take the other approach, focusing on the Scripture as an end in itself: "I am so glad you have a Bible and are reading it. Believe it, young man. It is the word of God. Believe it. Read it. And you will never go wrong."

Philip was wise. He understood the importance of the written word for what it is. "Then Philip began to speak, and starting with this scripture, he proclaimed to him the good news about Jesus" (Acts 8:35). He did not give the eunuch information. He gave him Jesus. The purpose of Scripture is not information—it is transformation in Christ.

We have been trained in our seminaries to approach the Scriptures from a historical-critical perspective. Our heads have been stuffed full of information which we bring back to our people, but information does not give life. I have visited many Sunday school classes when the people were going through their quarterlies, studying the lives of Abraham, Moses, David, or one of the other biblical characters. Information is given bout 4,000-year-old people, and we feel that the purpose of the class has been accomplished. Scripture was not given for information. It was given that we might see the One who is the author of life and be radically transformed through him.

We find Christ through the Scripture as we can in no other way. Luke records these words of Jesus to his disciples after the resurrection: "These are my words that I spoke to you while I was still with you—that everything written about me in the law of Moses, the prophets, and the psalms must be fulfilled." Then he opened their minds to understand the scriptures (Luke 24:44-45).

The disciples had grown up steeped in the history, tradition and information of the Scriptures. Jesus took them past the information to the place of understanding—the place of transformation.

Doers of the Word

Be doers of the word, and not merely hearers who deceive themselves. (James 1:22)

Isaiah was ministering in Judah when the people were going through a "heightened religious interest" phase. The people were returning to the temple in great numbers. There was a resurgence of emphasis on personal piety. People were praying and fasting again. Bible study, family values, and personal morality were the order of the day. Some would have called what was happening "renewal." The people were attending Bible studies and filling their notebooks full of information— but they stopped short of transformation. They wondered why God didn't hear their prayers.

God tells Judah, through the prophet Isaiah, that true renewal demonstrates itself in our relationships with people. People moved by God's Spirit will be involved with the oppressed, hungry, and homeless poor. People who are informed by the Word of God will be held accountable for living the whole justice of God.

> Is not this the fast that I choose:
>   to loose the bonds of injustice,
>   to undo the thongs of the yoke,
> to let the oppressed go free,
>   and to break every yoke?
> Is it not to share your bread with the hungry,

and bring the homeless poor into your house;
  when you see the naked, to cover them,
    and not to hide yourself from your own kin?
Then your light shall break forth like the dawn,
  and your healing shall spring up quickly.

(Isaiah 58:6-8*a*)

During the fall of 1979, the people of Ginghamsburg Church decided that we needed to practice what we were learning from God's Word. It was clear that renewal and involvement with hurting people had a direct correlation. We started the "adopt a Christmas family" program, which involved the commitment to spend on a family in need the same amount we would spend on our own family. In the past, many of us had simply gone to the local discount store and spent $5.00 or less on a cheap toy or pair of mittens, wrapped them, and then dropped the package in a barrel in the hallway of the church. Or worse yet, some had brought an old doll from home—one with crayon marks and half the hair missing—and given it in the name of Christian love. Let's be honest. That is not love—that is cleaning out the garage.

The leading of the Spirit was clear. If you bought your child a new bike, you would buy another child a new bike. Why was a used bike good enough for someone else's child, if it wasn't good enough for your own? If you bought your child name-brand clothes, then you would buy another child name-brand clothes.

All of us were assigned names and went to meet our "adopted" families around Thanksgiving time. The shopping adventure began as we set out with names, sizes, and wish lists. Most of us delivered our gifts on Christmas Eve.

When we all assembled in our little red brick and frame country church for the 11:00 P.M. candlelight service, you could sense a feeling of euphoria. As we sang our Christmas carols, we knew that we had truly acted Christian!

Do you know what God had the nerve to say to us?:

55

"You hypocrites! How dare you think that you are loving with the love of my Son, when you love with sacrificial love only one day out of 365! If you are truly my disciples, you will be involved with these people 365 days a year!"

"What are you saying, Lord—all 365 days? Why, Lord, that means that they will have to have my telephone number!"

But that is exactly what it means! Loving with Christ's love means that when I buy my kids' back-to-school clothes, I will buy my Christmas family back-to-school clothes too. When I send my two kids to camp, I will send my Christmas family's kids to camp. When our daughter, Kristen, had braces put on her teeth, we made the commitment to help a young college student get braces. This lifestyle of giving can be pretty scary. My son just got braces!

Renewal broke out at our church when the people began to actively do what we had been reading in God's written Word. Jesus was taking us past the *information* to the place of *transformation*.

Tom and Lisa Jelenek came to Ginghamsburg shortly after they were married in 1983. Tom is an environmental specialist with a large company, and Lisa teaches French at one of the area high schools. Tom made a commitment to Jesus as Savior and Lord during his first year at Ginghamsburg, and both he and Lisa began to grow in Christian discipleship.

Through their newly discovered practice of Bible reading, they began to develop a deeper sense of responsibility toward meeting the needs of others. Tom became deeply involved in our mission outreach programs. In fact, many of our mission ministries began under Tom's direction. One Thanksgiving, he worked with a mission team that rebuilt houses in South Carolina following Hurricane Hugo.

Lisa began a friendship with a woman who had been in and out of several disastrous marriages, the victim of abusive and codependent relationships since childhood. Tom and Lisa helped her become reestablished in a new apartment. They welcomed her often into their home, brought her to church, and helped her get through nursing school. Why?

"I just couldn't help it," Lisa said. "It was the Holy Spirit. When I looked at this woman who had been abused by her husband and had nowhere to go . . . I just had to help. I looked at everything we had and the very little that she had. The Spirit helped me get beyond my materialistic lifestyle to reach out to someone in need."

It is the business of the church to enable people to come to this point of biblical understanding, where transformation results. This was my first priority when I came to Ginghamsburg Church. I encourage people to bring their Bibles to worship. We look at the different passages together. The people make notes, underline passages, and ask questions. The Bible once again has become the chief source in our Sunday school classes. I have taught the Trinity Bible Study series on Wednesday nights since 1982, and as people become more exposed to the message of this unique book, they become more focused in their commitment to Christ and his church. They move out of the pew and on to the playing field. Rugged individualism and self-centeredness is replaced with a sense of true community. Dead organizations become living organisms. Closed minds give way to the mind of Christ. Prejudice and judgment yield to justice and active love.

Renewal depends upon the local church rediscovering the vital, unique truth that God has given us in this book. The Scripture must be seen as the primary source for determining all matters of faith and practice in our spiritual journeys. As Saint John of the Cross so aptly stated, "If we are guided by divine Scripture we shall not be able to err, for he who speaks in it is the Holy Ghost.[4]

CHAPTER III

THE LITURGICAL PRINCIPLE

We need new wineskins to hold new wine.
- Relate worship forms to the needs of the unchurched.
- Worship needs to be relevant to lifestyle.

You can batten down . . . just like a voice echoing through a cave . . . you can enjoy your classic worship in this cathedral. But this is not where this culture is. The Spirit of God is moving out there.[1]

Leonard Sweet

Martin Luther was sitting in a German beer garden, surrounded by baskets of red and white geraniums hanging from wooden beams. The tables were occupied by college students who had evaded their afternoon classes to find refreshment in the midst of the afternoon heat. He looked with deep passion into the faces of these young people, who had so quickly neglected the eternal for the sake of temporal economic dreams and humanistic philosophies. He contemplated ways to bridge the cavernous gap between the message of Jesus and the cultural identity of these students.

On this particular humid afternoon, the students seemed to be in an especially good mood as they sang a college song and lifted their mugs of hefeweizen beer. Luther listened intently. Walking home through the street lined with red-roofed houses, he couldn't seem to get the melody out of his head. He would repeatedly find himself humming it. "That's it!" It was as if the idea had come directly from heaven.

Luther was so concerned with finding ways to reach those young college students that he put the gospel message into popular music form. Historians are not certain whether Luther composed the tune for the hymn "A Mighty Fortress Is Our God," but it is well documented that many of Luther's hymns were inspired by the "beer garden" music of his day.

> [Luther's] tunes were largely made up of phrases from plainsong or adaptations of current songs, some of which were already associated with sacred words and some with secular. He was chided for going so far afield as to bring folk songs into the sanctuary. . . . And the practical effect of Luther's course was not to secularize church song so much as to turn the current of German music into a religious channel. . . . The twice-told tale of his phenomenal success in making popular song his agent in spreading the gospel and heartening the gospelers does not need to be repeated here.[2]

Renewal gives birth to new worship forms, which relate to the needs and culture of unchurched people rather than to the preferences of the churched. Jesus said that he came to "seek out and to save the lost" (Luke 19:10). This same mission becomes the primary focus of both the church and the forms of worship in renewal.

Relating to the Needs of the Unchurched

John Wesley was comfortable in the high church setting and was committed to his formal, liturgical Anglican background. This presented a rather complex dilemma when the pulpits of the Church of England began to close to him, because of his newly found experience in Christ and his emphasis on salvation by faith. He found his audience, almost by default, to be made up primarily of the unchurched working class. It didn't take

Wesley long to see that the traditional way of doing things wasn't going to work. The liturgy and hymnody were irrelevant to the unchurched crowds, who would often jeer and shout obscenities. Some would stop and briefly listen, but Wesley could not seem to keep their attention long enough to reach their hearts with the gospel.

John said to his brother Charles, "Chuck, that German music is too heavy and not melodic enough for the English coal miners. Go out and listen to the workers sing as they go back and forth to the mines, and then sit down and write something that will reach their hearts."

Charles Wesley's work put the gospel message into a "Top 40" format. He wrote "folk music" for the sake of relating the gospel to the hearts of the unchurched masses. He felt that his music was not reverent enough to be used in the formal worship of the church; it was intended to be used only for the informal house meetings. The institutional church of his day never accepted his style.

The Methodist renewal was born out of the contemporary music forms of Wesley's day. As the gospel becomes relevant to the unchurched through their own indigenous cultural forms, they begin to flood the church, to the extent that they become more numerous than the churched. The informal then replaces the formal and becomes the new liturgical form. This is a critical renewal principle. The church always adopts the worship forms of the last renewal movement. It is currently using worship forms that are 125 to more than 250 years old. We may update the words and images in the new book of worship, but the wineskins are still old and brittle. It is time to get new wineskins!

Wesley's goal was to reach the heart of the unchurched people. That's also the agenda of Jesus. Jesus didn't come to cater to the preferences of the churchgoers. He came to meet the needs of the unchurched. And this must be our agenda, too!

Worship That Makes Sense

We were created to worship. Worship is that place where we get in touch with God's presence and discover anew who we are. Through worship, our spirits are energized and our priorities realigned. Worship is meant to be at the heart of life, but often has been presented in a way that is divorced from life.

I was speaking in a large "oldstream" church recently. During the worship time, I saw boredom and indifference written all over the faces of yawning people. Many were just going though the motions of reciting ancient, tired rituals. Up, down. Up, down.

"Didn't we just sit down?" wonders a mother as she wrestled with her struggling two-year-old and tried to juggle her bulletin and hymnal. Somehow the Apostles' Creed does not seem relevant to the moment.

I know these yawning people get excited about other things. I have witnessed their zealous enthusiasm at athletic events, Rotary clubs, and sales meetings. Yet we can be so apathetic about worship. We wonder where our young people have gone. Most of our churches are perceived as offering worship that is irrelevant to our everyday lives. The worship bulletin may announce that the organ prelude is "Preghiera in E" by Oresta Ravenello, but what difference does that make? People are looking for something fresh and vital. The worship experience must make sense to them.

In my first year of ministry at Ginghamsburg Church, I was visiting the home of one of our older members who was convinced that the contemporary music we were using on Sunday morning was "inappropriate for God's house." He was passionately pleading the case for adhering to the sacred hymnody and traditions of the church.

"Pastor," he said as he cleared his voice, "how can God be happy with this hippity-hop music? People even want to clap their hands. It just isn't being respectful to God to clap in church."

I happened to notice that he had quite an extensive record collection, and I asked what he might have in the way of sacred hymns. His response didn't surprise me. He was an avid collector of the big-band era, with such names as Benny Goodman, Stan Kenton, George Getz, and Duke Ellington, but he didn't have a single album of sacred hymnody in this collection! He was pleading the cause of the importance of the traditional hymns, but his collection betrayed his first love in music.

Why do we cling to worship forms that are so formal, when our everyday lives are so informal? Sometimes we try to force on others what doesn't even work for ourselves. Many of our theological terms and phrases do not make sense to unchurched people. For them, sitting through a worship service is like listening to the technological jargon of a surgeon or a rocket propulsion expert. Worship must relate to the nitty-gritty places of ordinary people in everyday life. We cannot make sense of what we have not experienced.

As our American pioneer culture moved westward, the Methodists and Baptists were masters at relating the gospel to a resistant unchurched culture. They were instrumental in the Second Great Awakening because of their effective use of hard hitting, relevant preaching, common-sense worship, and up-beat music.

Peter Cartwright, one of the great frontier preachers, claimed that "the great mass of our western people wanted a preacher that could mount a stump, a block, or old log, or stand in the bed of a wagon, and without note or manuscript, quote, expound, and apply the word of God to the hearts and con-sciences of the people."[3]

The music and worship forms of the rapidly growing frontier church were vastly different from those of the eastern churches, which held to highly institutional and formal services. The music was essentially "folk" music. The worship "was crude and direct."[4] This make-sense approach of frontier worship, di-rected at the heart of an unchurched audience, is one of the primary reasons we find Baptist or Methodist churches in most of the counties in the United States.

Worship is one of the most important experiences we have together as a community of faith. It must be vital and relevant to people in the context of their life situations. We need to work hard at not letting it become drab, routine, or boring.

Vital Worship

At Ginghamsburg, we assemble worship teams comprised of people who play synthesizers, guitars, flutes, horns, cellos, drums, and a variety of other instruments. Not only does this better reflect the music of our contemporary culture, but it gives many more people an opportunity to participate in worship by using their gifts and talents. How many baby boomers have a guitar tucked away in a closet somewhere? One of our Sunday school classes is geared toward people interested in playing in the church orchestra. Another is designed around the youth praise team. These classes attract people according to their interests, and make wise use of their time for people with very hectic lifestyles.

As a leadership team, we talk about and evaluate worship every week. It is very important that the celebration of worship doesn't become predictable and routine. Nontraditional orders of worship can fall into the rut of predictability just as quickly as more traditional styles. We make use of creative calls to worship, drama, times of prayer, and opportunities for people to share personal expressions about their faith journeys. It is important to use a variety of prayer experiences, including conversational prayer and small-group prayer circles. The people of God will never learn to be the priesthood of God if all we ever use are pastoral prayers.

People need to be players in the worship experience, not just spectators. On several occasions, I have begun worship by asking someone to call us to worship by sharing significant Scripture passages they have found particularly meaningful during the previous week. They then stand up and share a brief verse or two. The worship team, of eight to twenty members, then leads everyone in a time of worship and praise. We usually sing four to six songs, the first usually very celebrative and upbeat, the last soft and reflective. This time of worship sometimes includes a traditional hymn, more often than not done in an untraditional way.

Usually the worship time is followed by a period of prayer, which might be conversational, or an individual might be called on to lead. The prayer time might have a theme such as thanksgiving, confession, or intercession. Sometimes we pray for those who express particular needs.

Personal faith stories help build faith. We often have a time of sharing in our order of worship for this purpose. Sometimes people are encouraged to stand and briefly share their witness from their seat. We also have people, with advance notice, share from the pulpit. Brevity must be considered, so we ask those who share from the pulpit to write their witness out first and limit it to three minutes. A staff person listens and helps them make adjustments ahead of time. We do not want to appear slick, but we are committed to excellence.

The time of sharing is followed by skits, special music, offering, ministry of the Word, and benediction. Sometimes the closing experience offers the people a moment to share "what I am hearing God say to me through this experience." The total worship celebration lasts about an hour.

I cannot overstate the importance of allowing worship to be unpredictable and people-involved.

"Your worship experience should not be totally dependent upon me," I said to the people at the opening of one of the worship celebrations. "The Bible says that each person should bring a unique gift to offer to God in the worship experience. One can bring a hymn, another can share a prayer, and someone else can offer a word of testimony."

I wasn't sure whether it was going to work. With hesitancy and reservation about the potential negative fallout, I struck out into an unpredictable, yet potentially promising learning experience. I said, "I am going to leave worship right now and go back and take care of the kids in the nursery."

Silence was the only response as I stepped off the platform and made my way down the aisle and out the back door of the small sanctuary. Would chaos ensue? I wondered to myself. Will the visitors come back? Will I still have a job next Sunday?

I listened intently to the small speaker box on the nursery wall that carried the sound of a murmuring audience from the sanctuary. It's not going to work. Now what? Suddenly the thought was interrupted by a familiar voice coming through the speaker box, the voice of Deane Loar:

"I know that you all might think this is silly, but I make up songs in the shower—songs for God."

With that, Deane began to sing for the congregation a song that he had written for God. Then he taught the people to sing it. It was simple, but the impact was humbling and powerful.

Len Kubal then came forward and read a particularly meaningful passage of Scripture that had confronted him during the week. Tom Sampley told about the devastating loss of his brother. The people ministered to him in prayer.

I didn't preach that weekend, but it probably is the most powerful message I have ever delivered.

All this change didn't occur at once. I had begun to use my guitar in worship when the organist quit. It was by accident that I first discovered the impact of contemporary music in worship! I was at Ginghamsburg seven years before worship teams were fully incorporated into our worship experience.

Communion is celebrated the first Sunday of every month, along with the invitation to prayer and the anointing with oil for those with needs for healing. These vehicles of grace often have been overlooked or downplayed in the church. We need to discover the presence of Christ anew through them.

Worship and Word

We must be sensitive to the "user-friendly" models of worship that are growing in popularity, without compromising the radical demands of the call of Christ in the name of relevancy. I often hear people say that they were attracted to Ginghamsburg Church because of the contemporary style of worship and preaching.

People are looking for a relevant word, but not a compromising word. They are listening for a clear word from God, in the midst of a labyrinth of theological and moral uncertainty. The churches that will offer new life and hope to this age will be the churches that have relevant worship styles, Christ-centered prophetic preaching, and social sensitivity.

What Makes Worship Vital?

What attracts people to a worship celebration? Why do they want to return? What makes worship vital? Here are some of the responses from people who were asked about their worship experience at Ginghamsburg Church:

"The very first time I entered this church, I had the feeling that something was different, something I never experienced in any other church. I couldn't put my finger on what this difference was right away. It wasn't until we became part of the church some months later that I realized that what I was experiencing, for the first time, was the Holy Spirit in action through the people there. They would love us. It was just a rather unusual feeling that I experienced the very first time that I came here."

"We came in, and it was kind of noisy, and there was a lot of life, and there were lots of people talking to each other, and, from my experience, a little bit of chaos."

"I saw people hugging each other. After church, people were standing around talking. That wasn't the type of church that I had gone to, where people left immediately after church was over."

"I think informal worship has definitely made an impact on my worship experience, because there is a freedom there that allows the Holy Spirit to just work in me."

"It is exhilarating for us to come together and collectively acknowledge Jesus as Lord. The testimonies of others heal me. I walk away and say 'yes, Lord, it's exciting to see how you are using your people.' The opportunity to just share life with one another in his presence is part of worship here."

Notice the emphasis placed upon worship that is experiential and relational, rather than worship that is informational and ritualistic. Words frequently used to describe worship include *experience, feeling, experiencing the Holy Spirit, action, love, relationships, hugging, talking, enjoying, freedom, exhilarating, collectively, testimonies, healing, exciting, sharing life, in his presence.* These people are talking about experiencing God and celebrating God's presence, as they celebrate and experience real life.

We are more than cerebral beings. We are whole persons. Vital worship must speak to the whole of human experience. It must reach into the physical, spiritual, relational, emotional, and rational dimensions of who we are as the people of Jesus, in a real world context. This type of worship continually calls us back to authentic living under the Lordship of Jesus Christ.

The district superintendent was visiting one of our three worship celebrations on a Sunday morning. He noticed immediately the informal dress of the predominantly baby-boomer-aged congregation as he entered the multipurpose room, where well over 400 people gathered in a space designed for 270. The room was vibrating with conversation, laughter, and anticipation. He sensed what some have described as a mild atmosphere of chaos, as people maneuvered their way through the crowd to get a cup of coffee, and ushers moved with efficiency to create extra space. He couldn't help noticing the enthusiasm and participation of the people in the worship experience, as contrasted to most of the churches in his district.

"Mike, I know this worship style is working for you," he commented. "But look at your congregation. It is so young! You have done a great job in reaching the baby-boomer generation in your geographic area. But what would you do if you were in an area where most of the people were older? What style of worship would you offer if you lived in a retirement area, like St. Petersburg, Florida?

"Dick," I replied, "If I lived in an area like St. Pete, on Sunday morning, I would offer the best big-band sound that you ever heard."

The agenda of Jesus is not the preference of the churched, but the needs of the unchurched. If the church is to experience a new movement of the Spirit, we need new worship forms to hold the new wine.

CHAPTER IV

THE COVENANT PRINCIPLE

Renewal involves commitment to the integrity of membership.
- Disciples? or Club members?
- Committed to Christ's purposes—reaching the lost and setting the oppressed free.
- Elevating membership standards heightens expectation and commitment.

The church is a covenant community, which means that there are gates. You know when you are in and when you are out of the community, even though the gospel issues a call to everyone. Jesus said, "If anyone would come after me, let them deny themselves, take up their cross and follow me." There is a sense in which following Jesus has an element of exclusiveness. We decide what not to follow in order to follow Christ, not just individually, but as part of the community. Every church has to wrestle with the cost of discipleship as it relates to being a part of this community of Jesus Christ.[1]

Howard Snyder

It costs something to be a follower of Jesus Christ. It costs something to be committed to his Body.

Whenever Jesus' message would begin to attract a large following, he would always blow it by saying something incredibly brash, even negative. He had a way of abruptly jarring people into the reality of what following him was all about.

> Whoever comes to me and does not hate father and mother, wife and children, brothers and sisters, yes, and even life itself, cannot be my disciple. (Luke 14:26)

> If any want to become my followers, let them deny themselves and take up their cross daily and follow me. (Luke 9:23)

> Foxes have holes, and birds of the air have nests; but the Son of Man has nowhere to lay his head. (Luke 9:58)

Are you ready to buy into that kind of itinerant lifestyle? Do you really understand with whom you are asking to become involved?

Jesus was always telling people to calculate the cost. He was not a pop psychologist, hawking a gospel of individualistic positive thinking. He was calling people to become part of a covenant community, a counter culture. Membership would involve forsaking individual goals and agendas for the sake of a higher purpose—the kingdom of God.

This call upset many of the institutionally religious. The author of the Gospel of John tells us that many of Jesus' disciples felt that his teaching was too "difficult"; "Because of this many of his disciples turned back and no longer went about with him" (John 6:66).

Many churches today see membership in the church in the same context as membership in a community club or organization. The church is just one of several organizations with which we are affiliated that has officers, committees, dinners, dues, and money-making projects. We give the church equal, or even less, priority than other responsibilities in our lives. Many approach scouting, youth sports, Rotary club, golf outings, and countless other activities with a greater zeal and intensity than any activity of the church.

The Son of God did not give his life for this institutional concept of church membership. It is far more costly to belong to the Body of Christ than to any other human organization. Like marriage, membership in Christ's Body is a covenant commitment. A covenant is different from institutional membership, in the sense that it is unbreakable. Unlike any other commitment we make, membership in Christ's Body is an eternal commitment.

The Membership Requirements at Ginghamsburg Church

When a church gets serious about renewal, it begins to ask new questions about the responsibilities of membership. Membership cannot and must not be separated from the cost of discipleship. Many people sense that there is no cost involved in their local church membership. Not much is expected. It is often harder to get into Cub Scouts than to become a member in many of our traditional church settings. At least, I had to go out and climb ten feet up a tree, acknowledged and signed off by my dad, to begin my journey into Scouts. My local church had no real expectation. At most, I was handed a box of offering envelopes.

The average attendance at Ginghamsburg exceeds membership by almost 500 people. A typical church in my denomination has a 39 percent ratio of attendance to membership. Attendance that is lower than membership is always the sign of a declining church. In renewal, the number of those coming to see what the Spirit of God is doing will always be greater than those who have accepted the commitment of covenant membership.

It costs something to be a follower of Jesus Christ. It costs something to be a member of his Body. When a person is seeking membership with Ginghamsburg Church, we ask them to spend three months in a class called Vital Christianity (see Appendix A). All missed classes must be made up, if the person is serious about pursuing membership. Attendance alone, however, does not insure membership. A person's commitment to the lordship of Jesus Christ, as evidenced by lifestyle integrity, is a primary consideration. Accepting the responsibilities and commitments of covenant membership through active stewardship, worship attendance, participation in a service-outreach ministry, and involvement in a small group is expected. The small group insures accountability and provides encouragement for spiritual growth. Jesus is calling disciples, not institutional members.

Our children pursue membership through this same process. A Vital Christianity class is offered for high school students. They do not go through a traditional confirmation experience prior to this time. Maturity and the understanding of covenant are important.

My daughter, Kristen, affirmed the covenant of membership at Ginghamsburg during her freshman year in high school. Prior to this "confirmation" experience she had participated in the building of two homes in Appalachia, worked on an inner-city project in Chicago, spent a week with a mission team in Jamaica, and worked for two years on an inner-city children's tutoring project in Dayton. She had also participated in a discipleship group since the seventh grade. We want our youth to have a sense of the servant lifestyle of followers of Jesus before they affirm a lifelong commitment to his church. Why rush people to the altar?

Each person is interviewed by a leadership team before he or she affirms the covenant of membership. Questions are concerning faith journey, the lordship of Christ, giftedness, service, small-group participation, and stewardship.

Attendance is tracked. People are contacted by letter or phone when they miss three weeks of worship. The membership roster is reviewed annually. Inactive members are contacted and asked about their intent to continue the covenant of membership at Ginghamsburg. They are encouraged to become active in their journey. If they cannot do this, they are asked to assume the relationship of "friend" to the congregation, until they can again actively reaffirm the covenant of a functioning member.

What Would John Wesley Say?

John Wesley's commitment to the covenant principle was crucial to the birth and vitality of the Methodist movement. Preaching and sacrament were not enough to renew old institutional bureaucracies and transform broken lives. People who were moved to commitment through anointed preaching tended to fall back into their old ways.

Wesley's genius lay in his ability to organize seekers and converts into vital discipleship groups called societies, classes, and bands. Each group represented a systematic, progressive step in spiritual maturity. If you were to be a member in the Methodist movement, you were expected to participate in a weekly group called a society. As the societies grew, they were subdivided into small groups of ten to twelve people called classes and bands. The leader of each class was responsible for the spiritual development of the members and for collecting money for the poor. Those who were unwilling to be committed to the cell group were discontinued from membership in the society. Tickets were given to those who were faithful; without a ticket, the member could not participate in the quarterly communion and love feast. If a member was not committed to the cell group during the second three-month period, his or her name was removed from membership in the Methodist society. Participation was not optional—it was expected.

The discipleship-accountability factor that Wesley's cell structure offered was the difference between those converts who continued to grow in their faith and commitment to

Christ's mission, and those who fell back into their old complacent ways (see Appendix B, "Rules of the Band").

We have found that people can find their way quickly out the back door of the church, if they don't become established in a small group after the process of membership. People stay in a church because they find fulfillment through significant relationships and responsibilities. Relationships are not formed in a crowd! The people who thrive in the ministry at Ginghamsburg are those who have made intimate friendships in HOME (Homes Open for Ministry and Encouragement) groups. These groups also provide a sense of healthy peer pressure, which reinforces growth and transformation in the new disciple.

Wesley understood that a church would be only as strong as its members. Institutional-club members breed institutionalism. Transformed-body members transform whole communities and cultures.

The Life of the Body Is in the Cell

Criticism and accusations did not stop Wesley's approach to covenant membership. A person who wanted to join the Methodist movement needed to first spend three months in a cell, where a well trained, mature leader taught the basics of the faith and discipleship. They could then be recommended for membership, but only on the condition that they were willing to submit themselves to the ongoing accountability and discipline of the cell. The disciple's continual involvement was evaluated quarterly. Each week, the members challenged one another's progress, in relation to spiritual maturity and involvement with the poor.

Wesley insisted that his people not divorce personal piety from social action. Many of his followers worked in soup kitchens, organized meals-on-wheels-type programs, and distributed clothing and medicine to the poor. Wesley understood that the best way to get close to God was not by our religious acts, but by our actions toward people. Your behavior with people, especially poor and disenfranchised people, gives you power with God (see Isaiah 58; Micah 6:6; John 13:35). Jesus said, "Just as you did it to one of the least of these who are members of my family, you did it to me" (Matt. 25:40). The test of authentic discipleship is what we do to people. Your actions and attitudes toward people are your actions and attitudes toward God.

> For I was hungry and you gave me food, I was thirsty and you gave me something to drink, I was a stranger and you welcomed me, I was naked and you gave me clothing, I was sick and you took care of me, I was in prison and you visited me. (Matt. 25:35-36)

Balanced discipleship takes place in the ongoing, nurturing environment of accountability provided by the cell group. Discipleship and discipline are one and the same. According to Robert Chiles:

> On many occasions, Wesley observed that the decline and deadness of a society was the result of disregard for discipline. He laments, "I met the classes; but found no increase in the society. No wonder, for discipline has been quite neglected; and, without this, little good can be done among the Methodists."[2]

For the purpose of vitality and accountability, membership progress was reviewed regularly. Covenant membership was not taken lightly in the early Methodist movement. There was no concept of lifelong institutional membership. Ongoing membership was based on accountability, discipline, progressive maturity, and involvement with the poor. Membership was reviewed and renewed quarterly.

Generally, people will give according to the level of expectation. Groups that expect more from people tend to get more. This can be seen in groups like the Mormons, where many of their young people give at least one year to full-time missionary service.

Covenant membership heightens expectation and commitment. In 1994, the 900 members of Ginghamsburg gave more than $2.2 million toward Christ's mission. Men and women will leave work early to drive a vanload of teenagers to one of our "Clubhouse" ministries, to work with children after school. Many more will spend much of their vacation serving Christ's purpose of reaching the lost and setting free the oppressed. Elevating the standards for membership elevates expectation and the quality of participation.

What Is a Body Life Member?

A Body life member is committed to Jesus Christ as Savior and Lord. Savior—that is the good news! Grace—the undeserved favor of God!

I was raised in the church, but I didn't understand until I was almost twenty years old that we don't earn God's favor by trying to be good people. We could never be good enough to meet God's standard. In Jesus Christ, God has done for us what we could never do for ourselves. He has made it possible for us to know that all our past, present, and future sins are forgiven. We can be certain that we will spend eternity in his presence. Christ shows us that nothing can separate us from God's love, not even our worst failures!

Our performance-oriented codependent culture needs to hear the good news of God's undeserved favor that can be discovered in his Son, Jesus Christ. Many of us who name Jesus as our Savior continue to jump through hoops of performance to earn the favor of God and others. This results in fragile self-esteem and unhealthy, codependent relationships. God's salvation in Christ is the truth that will bring health to our relationship with God, to our attitudes about ourselves, and to our relationships with others.

Jesus Christ does not just save us for heaven. He saves us to be fully human today. I was being interviewed by a reporter from the Dayton *Daily News* about the rapid growth of Ginghamsburg Church.

He asked me, "How do you keep your ego from running away from you?"

I replied, "That's easy. I know what I have the potential to become." The temptations that invade my thought life with varying degrees of intensity show my potential to have the morality of my schnauzer. I need a Savior who saves me from my darkest possibilities and allows me to have the integrity to be a faithful husband and father today.

I enjoy nice things—nice suits, expensive ties, designer jeans, classic cars—they clamor for my energies. Forty thousand people die every day on this planet from lack of food. Forty thousand people a day, and I am thinking about *things!* I need a Savior today to save me from my selfishness and turn me outward to be a servant to others. I need a Savior to save me from the golden calf of consumerism.

To be a member of Christ's Body means that you recognize him as Lord. *Lord* means absolute authority—owner. Periodically, I teach a course at a local seminary. In that class, I had been talking about the concept of slave, as it related to the lordship of Jesus Christ. Volunteerism is the language of the club. Slave is the language of the kingdom of God.

One of the women came up to me just before class and boldly asserted, "If you use that word 'slave' one more time, I am going to get up and walk out. Slave has a negative connotation in our culture today." I was momentarily startled. Her comment really bothered me. But after some reflection, it occurred to me that the word *slave* has always had a negative connotation. It has not been a popular occupation in any culture. A slave is not something that anyone ever wanted to be, but it is the only word that lets me know that I am no longer in charge of my own destiny.

Martin Luther said that when Christians get out of bed in the mornilng, the first words out of their mouths should be "I am baptized." *Baptized* means dead, buried, and out of the way, so that God can inhabit my body and do with me as he pleases. It is like something out of the *Invasion of the Body Snatchers.* It looks like me and sounds like me, but it really is only my body, invaded by the Holy Spirit, perpetrating the reality of God's kingdom. God has access to all my possessions, bank accounts, and relationships. *Baptized* means dead to my agendas, prejudices, and perceptions, but alive to the will and actions of Christ.

Too many of us bring our own agendas and prejudices to the places where decisions are made in our churches. Our decisions reflect the values of our culture, rather than the kingdom of God. We vote our Republican or Democratic agendas, our liberal or conservative persuasions. We must empty ourselves of everything, so that we can truly reflect the mind of Christ. Only then will the world look at the Church and see a movement which mirrors the kingdom of God, not the prevailing culture.

A story is told about a group of Mennonites in Vietnam during the Vietnam war. Mennonites are pacifists, and they had been ministering in the country for years, trying to win the Vietnamese to Jesus. When the war broke out, they continued their efforts, providing food and medical supplies to people in both North and South Vietnam.

The American government attempted to have them moved out of North Vietnam, stating that for an American citizen to aid the enemy during war time is equivalent to being a traitor to their country. The Mennonite reply was significant: "We are citizens of the kingdom of God, and our allegiance is to our King. Our King says 'When your enemy hungers, feed them.' " When we accept Jesus Christ as our Lord and Savior, our allegiance to him is higher than to anyone else. Jesus Christ must be the supreme authority in our lives.

Do you accept Jesus Christ as your Lord and Savior and pledge your allegiance to his kingdom? This means that you can have no higher allegiances in your life. Your allegiance to Christ and his kingdom must supersede your allegiance to country, family, or vocation. To follow Jesus and enter into a covenant relationship with his Body means that he is your highest authority.

A Body Life Member is
Connected to Christ's People

One of the tragic heresies in the church today is the individualistic attitude that it can be just me and Jesus—me and Jesus and the TV.

The Church as the Body of Christ is a living organism, not an organization. I cannot be connected to the Head if I am disconnected from the Body, and I cannot be connected to the Body if I am disconnected from the Head. Juan Carlos Ortiz reminds us that our elbows are members of our bodies because they are connected and functioning. The elbow receives instruction from the head and passes instruction on. It receives nourishment and passes nourishment on. It is not a member because its name is on a list of the body members.

A covenant member accepts all the responsibilities and liabilities that go with Christ's mission. If you are not receiving instruction from the Head and passing instruction on, you are not a Body member. If you are not receiving nourishment and passing nourishment on, you are not functioning as a member of the Body of Christ.

When I accepted Jesus as Lord of my life, I was born into his Body, the Church. You cannot commit your life to Jesus and not become an active part of the Body. The Church is the living presence of Christ in the world. To be committed to Christ is to be connected and functioning with his people. Covenant members must no longer make excuses for not supporting Christ's mission with money, time, prayer, and service. Covenant members must be dead, buried, and free from the priorities and goals of the world. Christ must have full access to all that they are and all that they have. They must be fully committed to his purpose of reaching the lost and setting free the oppressed.

As members of the Body of Christ, we are the only hands, feet, mouthpiece, and bank account that Jesus has on this earth. Membership is that place in one's spiritual pilgrimage where we say "I do" to this responsibility. The sacrament of baptism is not enough to define the role of membership. We cannot carry someone to commitment. Each person must give his or her own response to the command, "Follow me."

It costs something to be a follower of Jesus Christ. In times of renewal, the Church rediscovers this important principle. The integrity of membership cannot be divorced from the cost of discipleship. Jesus is calling disciples, not club members.

CHAPTER V

THE PRIESTHOOD PRINCIPLE

Equipping laity for ministry is crucial in renewal.
- Helping people identify God's call.
- The church functions as a seminary.
- Throwing gasoline on burning bushes

Churches need to be allowing their lay people to be in ministry. They need to be stretching them. They need to be teaching them. They need to be challenging them. They need to give them that chance to fail. . . . I'm so thankful for the chance I had. It changed my life.

Sharon Amos,
Member at Ginghamsburg Church

The Business of the Church

So much of our energy in the church is spent in meetings, where we plan dinners and bazaars, and discuss such critical issues as what color to paint the fellowship hall. What really is the business of the church?

The apostle Paul, in the fourth chapter of Ephesians, tells us that Christ gave some to be apostles, some to be prophets, some to be evangelists, and some to be pastors and teachers, for the purpose of preparing God's people for the work of ministry. This is the primary business of the church—to enable our people to know Jesus as Lord, and then to equip them for ministry.

The New Testament church did not have seminaries for the privileged few to attend in order to become professionals, and then return to minister to spectators. Many of our people who sit in committees are not "doing" ministry. At best, they are only approving ministry for the professionals to carry out.

I recently talked to a young family man who had left his former church to come to Ginghamsburg Church.

"I have grown tired of sitting in meetings that have nothing to do with the kingdom of God," he told me with a sense of resolve. "I have spent the last year and a half of my life on a worship committee that has done nothing more than bicker about replating the cross above the altar. One faction wants to redo it in brass, citing cost and durability as the consideration. The other half of the group wants it plated in gold."

Haven't most of us served on a committee like that at one time or another? This project could have been entrusted to one capable person in the congregation, who could have done the job quickly, without wasting valuable frontline-mission time in the lives of others.

The New Testament church functioned as a seminary that raised up the laity from the inside, then turned them loose on the outside. When Paul wanted to establish a new church, he evangelized, established the new believers in the faith, equipped them for ministry, and then moved on to repeat this process in another place. When he left, a bishop didn't reappoint a new pastor from another church, nor did the church form a pastoral search committee. The pastors came from the local church body. The church functioned as a seminary, equipping its own people for the purpose of frontline mission.

The church in renewal rediscovers this important New Testament principle—the priesthood of all believers. There is no special caste system under the new covenant such as the Levitical priesthood in the old. All those who name Jesus as Lord are priests. All of us are called to be co-laborers in his mission in the world. This principle lies at the heart of every renewal movement throughout the history of the church. Releasing the laity for ministry in the world is the key to the success of Christ's mission.

In the eighth chapter of Acts, we read about the first great persecution experienced by the church: "That day a severe persecution began against the church in Jerusalem, and all except the apostles were scattered throughout the countryside of Judea and Samaria" (Acts 8:1). The apostles were the professional pastors. Later in that passage, we read: "Now those who were scattered went from place to place, proclaiming the word" (8:4).

What was the secret behind the early church's success in spreading the gospel to the uttermost parts of the earth? The laity had been equipped to be ministers and to proclaim the word, so the professionals remained in Jerusalem, where they continued to equip others for ministry in Jesus' name. The gospel was spread by the lay people!

This principle was at the heart of the Protestant Reformation. Luther reaffirmed this new covenant strategy—that there is but one high priest, Jesus, and all of us are priests, ministering in the same body under his authority.

We need to be careful in labeling the different ministry functions in the church. Our labeling systems tend to separate the clergy from the laity. At Ginghamsburg Church, we don't use the title "minister" to make a distinction between our professional clergy and the laity. All of us are ministers. I don't say that I am a minister and you are a layperson. I am a pastor. A pastor has a *function* in the body, not a position. A pastor has a function in the same sense that a person with the gift of teaching, or someone with the gift of administration has an important function. There is only one *position* defined in the body, and the one who holds that position is Jesus Christ, the head.

The Distinction Becomes Blurred

> Once we start trying to say "This is your sphere, clergy" and
> "this is your sphere, laity," for me, it is always a sign of . . . a
> dying church. A church that has the time to try and do those
> rigid definitions is a church collapsing into itself. If you are out
> there spreading the gospel of Christ and infiltrating the culture
> with that gospel, you don't have time to make those kinds of
> definitions. You are out there working, arm in arm, hand in
> hand. There is a renewed sense of the priesthood of all believers,
> and that is absolutely vital and essential for the renewed church.[1]
>
> Leonard Sweet

Someone recently asked me, "Who are the professional
pastors around here, anyway?" When the church is at its best,
you can't tell the professionals from the rest of the players.

John Wesley capitalized on this principle when he sent "lay"
circuit riders throughout the British Isles, and then across the
continent of North America. Most Methodist churches saw the
circuit rider only once a quarter. The circuit rider would serve
the sacraments and take care of weddings. The lay people
carried on the business of worship, teaching, evangelism, and
social ministries the rest of the time. They continued with
worship, Sunday school, and mission work on the weeks when
the professional pastor was not there.

The Baptist and Methodist movements saw incredible
growth during the Second Great Awakening. One reason you
see United Methodist and Baptist churches in almost every
county in the United States today is because of their depen-
dence upon the laity. The Methodist movement spread westward through the circuit rider, who lacked formal training by
professional standards. The Baptists grew through the farmer
who farmed by day and functioned as a lay pastor at night.

Those churches that made a clear distinction between the
professional clergy and laity, and emphasized a high standard
of educational training for the clergy, remained in the east, for
the most part. Not much happened in Episcopal and Congre-

gational churches during the Second Great Awakening, because of their focus on "professional" ministry.

Organic Ministry

Look at the way God has spread his gifts throughout the church:

> To each is given the manifestation of the Spirit for the common good. To one is given through the Spirit the utterance of wisdom, and to another the utterance of knowledge according to the same Spirit, to another faith by the same Spirit, to another gifts of healing by the one Spirit, to another the working of miracles, to another prophecy, to another the discernment of spirits, to another various kinds of tongues, to another the interpretation of tongues. All these are activated by one and the same Spirit, who allots to each one individually just as the Spirit chooses. . . . Indeed, the body does not consist of one member but of many. (1 Cor. 12:7-11, 14)

There are no superstars in the Body of Christ. Not one of us has all the gifts. I am limited in what I can do in ministry. God has gifted me to lead and to teach biblical truth in relevant ways, but I don't have other "pastoral" gifts that many would expect the "professional minister" to have. Many expect the professional pastor to function as a personal chaplain, hired to do everything. This professional model of ministry is not biblical.

We are meant to function in interdependent relationships with one another, as the Spirit works through us. This is an organic model of ministry. Each of us has a different function in the Body. One function is not more important than another. We have been baptized by the same Spirit and all are part of the same Body. But there are "varieties of activities."

When the bishop placed his hands upon me and ordained me to the ministry of word, sacrament, and order, it did not give me more of the Spirit, an elevated calling over the "nonordained," or anything that God had not already given me or called me to do.

God has set each of us apart and consecrated us for his purpose in the Body of Christ. For the Body to function according to God's purpose, each member must be encouraged to function as God's priest. The church must intentionally help people identify God's call. Equipping the saints for the work of ministry—this is the business of the church!

The Chicken-Parts Expert

I first met Sharon Amos when her daughter, Kim, began coming to the youth group during her freshman year in high school. We were planning a summer mission trip, and I had a meeting with parents to explain the purpose of the trip and share my expectations. After that meeting, Sharon told me that she was going to be married in a few weeks and move south of the Dayton area. Kim would not be able to participate in the youth program because of the distance.

The first Sunday morning after the wedding, Kim got up at 6:30 A.M. and went to the room of her mom and new stepdad.

"Mom, wake up! Will you give me a ride to the Dayton Mall, where I can catch a bus to Vandalia, and then get a ride with one of my friends to Ginghamsburg Church?"

Sharon could not believe what she was hearing, but she got up and drove her daughter to the mall, where Kim caught a bus, rode twenty-eight miles to Vandalia, and met a friend who drove her the remaining five miles to the church.

The next Sunday morning, the same scenario unfolded at 6:30 A.M.

Sharon assured herself that this would be a three- or four-week fad at most, but Kim's Sunday morning ritual continued for three months. The Amoses finally decided to get up and bring Kim themselves, to see what kind of "organization" had such a grip on their daughter.

They came out of curiosity, but soon became convinced that the message of Jesus they heard at Ginghamsburg Church was worth not only the drive, but the way of life. Sharon and Wayne grew to understand that belief equals commitment, which equals service. Both began to use their gifts and talents in serving Christ's mission. They started by traveling with the teens on mission work projects. They worked in Mexico, Chicago, New York City, and Pittsburgh. Half of their vacation time was committed to mission trips.

Sharon began teaching Sunday school, leading discipleship groups, and going on every possible youth trip. She also had the responsibility of a full-time job. She was a chicken-parts expert. I am not exactly sure what this involved, but it was related to the food brokerage industry and restaurant sales. Sharon eventually dropped to part-time status in her professional job, in order to donate twenty hours a week to our youth ministry team.

God had given Sharon a vision. She had seen God's burning bush. After working with Habitat for Humanity and other building projects in various cities, Sharon and Wayne began the Dayton work project, a ministry that involved insulating, painting, and rehabilitating housing for low-income families. They rented a dorm at Wright State University and held work camps for youth who came for a week at a time and grew in their faith in Jesus while serving others. The project ran for five weeks that first summer.

At the end of the five-week period, I began to get phone calls from other churches around the state, asking if Sharon Amos could come and be their youth minister. Sharon had never been to seminary! She was a chicken-parts expert! But she moved on from Ginghamsburg Church to become the youth minister at a church in West Carrollton.

The church must function as a seminary that equips the laity for the mission of Christ.

Developing the Curriculum

A seminary has a curriculum. If the local church is going to be a seminary that equips laity for ministry, then we need to be serious about developing a curriculum that will give lay ministers the necessary skills and knowledge for mission.

Our whole strategy of ministry at Ginghamsburg is focused on this ministry of equipping. (This strategy is discussed further under the Leadership Principle in the next chapter.) We have built our curriculum through the following areas:

Vital Christianity

This is our 13-week membership class that focuses on basic Christianity. The first third of the class deals with the person of Jesus Christ, his claims, his purpose, and his authority. The rest of the course deals with the Holy Spirit, spiritual gifts, Christian growth, and the meaning of covenant membership. Commitment to the Lordship of Jesus Christ, the ability to clearly articulate the gospel, a servant lifestyle, and visible commitment to the local church—these are essential entry points for the person who will serve in ministry. (See Appendix A: Vital Christianity Course Outline.)

Sunday School

Most of our classes are electives that change every quarter. At least one-third of these classes are designed for equipping people for particular ministries. There are classes for youth counselors, Sunday school teachers, small-group leaders, and various other ministries. Sunday school teachers take a training class during a quarter when they are not teaching.

Special Training Events

An example of this would be the weekend retreat for all people in teaching ministries. We bring in education specialists in the areas of preschool, elementary, youth, and adult ministries. We also sponsor an annual leadership retreat for all the leaders in the church. This is an important time for me to share my continued vision for the mission of Ginghamsburg Church with those who are so essential to its success.

Ministry Area

Each ministry area in our church has a particular strategy for discipleship. The Stephen ministers (lay care and counseling) go through a two-year weekly training process. At the end of that time, they are consecrated for ministry.

Weekend Conferences

These conferences cover such topics as healing, ministry to persons and families of persons with AIDS, cell-group ministry, divorce recovery, renewal, and single ministries.

Trinity Bible Series

This is a ten-semester Bible survey course designed to help Christians become biblically literate. We encourage all our people to take at least the first two semesters, Old and New Testament survey. Many other resources are available, such as *Bethel Bible Series* and *Disciple.*

On-the-Job Training

There is no better way to learn than by hands-on experience. Our people are first tested as workers before they are given the responsibility of leadership. This takes place through a mentoring process. A person first works as an assistant teacher, as an apprentice cell-group leader, or as a helper at youth functions on Sunday evenings or on mission trips. This approach allows people to grow into ministry and gives leadership ample time for observation.

Sending Laity to Key Training Events

Most pastors are given money for continuing education. If pastoral ministry and lay ministry are equal, then we must budget money for lay continuing education. Every year, we send a group of youth counselors to the Youth Specialties national convention. We have sent laity to Fuller Institute training events in California. If it is the business of the church to equip laity for the purpose of ministry, then we must invest in the education of the laity.

Accountability

If our commitment to the priesthood principle is to have vital consequences, one area that we cannot overlook is accountability. People who accept the high calling of Christ must be equally willing to accept this high standard. We cannot approach ministry with the idea that "I am a volunteer, so you should be thankful for anything I am willing to give." Christ does not call volunteers. He calls servants. These servants are people who are actively hearing God's call and following Jesus in the way of the cross. By the very act of following Christ, they have committed themselves to his standard of social and moral integrity. They are fully invested, with their time and resources, in Christ's mission of winning the lost and setting the oppressed free.

The people we recruit for ministry need to understand this standard up front. It is better to let a position go unfilled than to recruit a lukewarm person. Our ministry standard and expectation is clearly explained before a person begins his or her ministry (see Appendix C, the Teacher's Covenant). The Teacher's Covenant is presented to all teachers at Ginghamsburg Church before they begin their teaching ministry. It indicates our expectations, our commitment, and the accountability factor that we maintain.

But I'm Just an Ordinary Person . . .

As you have been reading along, have any of the following thoughts crossed your mind?:

Ginghamsburg Church has really gotten its act together, and everything is working well there. The professional ministers place trust in the laity. They practice the priesthood of all believers, and laypeople are encouraged and supported in ministry. Ginghamsburg Church utilizes a curriculum for strengthening lay ministry and has an accountability structure in place. They have exceptional lay people like Sharon Amos, a person with vision, who knows her function in the Body and has the knowledge and enthusiasm to do something with it. That's great for Ginghamsburg, but it would never work in my church. I go to an ordinary church, and I'm just an ordinary person.

Frequently I get feedback from visiting laypeople that involves a mixture of hope and perplexity. A typical visitor to our church might say something like this:

> I am fascinated and in awe of the tremendous variety of ministry that is occuring at Ginghamsburg Church. I wish we could do that in my church, but we simply don't have that kind of leadership, and we laypeople don't know how or where to begin on our own.

Visitors get excited because they like what they find at Ginghamsburg, and they want to carry their excitement back to their own church. Laity wants to be involved in meaningful ministry. Their questions impress me with their earnest desire to serve Christ more completely, hidden behind more direct questions: "Mike, how do I get started in my own church? How do I know that God is speaking to me? What could I do to bring this kind of new life into my congregation?" Visiting pastors have similar questions and comments:

> Mike, what I see happening at Ginghamsburg Church is my dream for my congregation. I am fascinated and in awe of the tremendous variety of ministry that is occurring here. I want to see my lay people more involved and on fire for Christ. I wish our church could develop new ministries like

Ginghamsburg has, but we simply don't have that kind of congregation. My members expect me to do the pastoral planning and ministry—it's just a different kind of place. This would never work in my congregation.

I began to wonder about these comments and asked a few questions of my own: "Does Ginghamsburg have exceptional people, or is our ministry carried on by ordinary people? Is Ginghamsburg really so different? How did all these extensive ministries get started?"

At Ginghamsburg Church, youth ministry is involved in day-to-day local-mission outreach, week-long mission trips, leadership training, and praise teams. It leads congregational worship several times a year and produces a top-notch drama production each year. Where did all this begin? How did Mike Nygren know that God wanted him to work in youth ministry? Do the people who are leading successful ministry areas at Ginghamsburg have some type of unique spirituality? Or are they just ordinary people? My mind began churning these questions, and I felt compelled to seek answers.

The business of the church is to know Jesus and to make him known to others. I know how professional pastors do this, but how does a layperson know that he or she is called to do a specific task? How do laypeople find their unique calls from Jesus and get started in ministry? Does God really speak to individuals, ordinary people, today? How do "ordinary people" hear God's direction? "There is only one thing to do," I thought to myself, "just ask the experts!"

Where Do I Find My Burning Bush?

It was not difficult to mentally identify some "burning bush experts" at Ginghamsburg. Looking at the existing ministry areas, and remembering the people instrumental in the beginning of each ministry, I came up with a few questions to ask—questions that other people ask me. My respondents are ordinary people. They have not gone to seminary. None has taken a course in "How to Begin a New Ministry." They were not given a list of things to do to begin a Clubhouse, a Kid's Camp, or a Women's Ministry. They are vastly different in personality and religious background, and they have profoundly different ideas about how to accomplish their goals.

Their common denominator is that they felt a need to pursue a certain ministry. They saw a burning bush. They had a vision for a particular ministry, to meet a particular need. God spoke to them in some manner, communicating to each of them God's plans, dreams, and visions. They all have a passion to serve Jesus, as he has shown them how and where to serve. And all of them heard a different call at Ginghamsburg.

Mike, our youth director, had this to share concerning his entrance into youth ministry and God's call upon his life for this ministry:

> If I was "called," there was no burning bush, no visible and outright affirmation to give up my painting business to pursue youth ministry, but rather I had this inner passion that recognized how God could use me in the lives of teens.

Carolyn's reply was similar. She listened to a verse that haunted her. She responded. And the early stages of a women's ministry came into existence:

> My vision for an active women's ministry originated on a walk around my neighborhood. Luke describes Jesus' challenge to enter into the harvesting process and asks us to join in as laborers in his harvest. That verse kept haunting me as I walked past the houses surrounding my own home.

Carolyn also spoke of our unique ministries, and the plans that God has for each of us. She went on to give instructions on hearing, responding to, and defining our unique roles:

> I believe that God creates each of us individually and uniquely, and deep within our makeup are the seeds of the ministry he has prepared for us. If we believe Psalm 139:13-16 and Jeremiah 1:4-5 and 29:11, then we know that God

has plans for us! Living a life of yieldedness and obedience, and listening for the voice of the Spirit, allows God to work those plans through us. I believe he matches us up according to temperaments, natural talents, interests, and spiritual gifts with the plan he has for us. In other words, he equips us to follow his call—even before we are born!

What actions did Carolyn take in the early stages of the present Women's Ministry?

I began a neighborhood Bible study for women, which grew from 9 participants to 30. Then we moved into the church, divided into several groups, and had 75 to 100 women involved in what became "Morning with a Purpose." From this beginning, we have grown to a ministry that affects more than 400 women, through a variety of ministries: retreats, "Evening with a Purpose," "Morning with a Purpose," Christian aerobics, a mentoring ministry, outreach to inner-city moms, and a planned outreach to preschool moms. The key has been to allow other women to see their own burning bushes—the place where they hear the voice of God calling them. Also significant is fostering their natural bent to ministry (interests, talents, and personalities), developing their spiritual gifts, and deepening their walk with Christ. The bottom line is putting it all under the rule and authority of Christ.

I asked Lou Walthall to relate the earliest memories of children's ministries at Ginghamsburg. Under Lou's leadership, ministry to children expanded and flourished, and new avenues of ministering to children were developed:

Since the early 1970s, I had dreamed of having my own preschool, but I never thought I'd have the opportunity for this dream to come true. I remember sharing this dream with Mike Slaughter, and he challenged me to not start "my" preschool, but to move toward a preschool that belonged to Jesus and was committed to making him the focus. It sounded good, but as I looked at the old church building, I knew that there was no way! Without the right facility, the dream was impossible. How wrong could I be?

Ginghamsburg Church seemed to be on the cutting edge in so many areas, but no one had a vision for helping children find Christ in a personal way and providing experiences so that they could grow in their relationship with him. I began to ask questions and make my concerns known. I could not have verbalized it at the time, but God was giving me that vision.

When I became children's ministry coordinator, I started to look at the needs of each age level and began developing ministries to meet those needs. Sitting at the kitchen table one day, I realized that this is different. This was no longer "doing my duty" for the church. This was God's plan for ministry!

I had no idea how big God's plan, his vision, could and would be! In 1984, we moved into the new discipleship center and Ginghamsburg Preschool opened its doors. We were thrilled with our 19 students. The school has served well more than 800 students since that time.

Mike Nygren had words of wisdom and stories about different areas of teen ministry and its development at Ginghamsburg. He spoke of how the teen mission plans developed, where the vision comes from, and our ability to dream God's dream:

The development of missions is a maturing process. We should start in our own backyard, making sure we really understand who we are as individuals, as a church, and as a community. We need to see what we are doing from the perspective of Jesus, and also what else needs to be done.

To dream, we must simply be open to listen to God. To accomplish the dreams, we must be willing to go where God leads us, even if it is new or alien to us.

For churches to develop an outward-journey strategy, they

need to be willing to think beyond what they already do or are comfortable with. Outward-journey ministry focuses on seeing the world's needs through the eyes of Jesus, and then working toward meeting those needs. The transforming part of our journeys has come through patience and perseverance, and by being attentive to the opportunities around us.

Mike spoke of the early Clubhouse ministries:

Our youth group is currently involved in an after-school ministry to 15 to 20 in the inner-city of Dayton. For 112 of the 180 school days of the year, our teens show up for this ministry. It's not easy to coordinate this ministry, but it works. I believe youth ministry has the opportunity to teach the values of life that we all need to have.

This after-school ministry began the first two years with one day a week. It progressed to two days a week, and finally, now, to four. The teens were encouraged to dream, and the dream turned into a reality. The reality today is a rented storefront which we renovated and now call the Clubhouse.

Another annual event, the Thanksgiving Dinner, regularly serves 400 people in need. The entire meal is planned and prepared by teens.

I thought of the Norman Rockwell image of Thanksgiving dinner, with a festive family around a table overflowing not only with food, but with love. So the dream was born to provide a dinner to our small community that would fill both of the needs that arise on Thanksgiving Day. We would be the families that many in the community were missing on Thanksgiving Day.

Why do we keep having the dinner year after year? I suspect that our guests find the holiday with us just a little more enjoyable, a little less lonely. And the teens could stay home all day, but I suspect that their lives also would be a little emptier. That is why we have the dinner every year, year after year.

One of our teens, Robin Gale, was featured in an article in a local newspaper. Robin was then a seventeen-year-old high school senior and a paid intern at the Clubhouse. She directed more than thirty teen volunteers in ministering to the local children in the after-school program. She also had served in Jamaica, Mexico, New York, and in other local projects. Robin states, "I'm the kind of person who needs to be doing something. It scares me to think what I'd be if I hadn't become a Christian and found a place to plug myself in."

Richard, a youth counselor who works with Mike Nygren, said this about the beginnings of Dream Builders, a ministry that restores dilapidated houses in the inner city:

I think the idea for a new ministry comes from within the Body, the church, as an outgrowth of something that is already happening. I see it as a group process, taking some involvement, improving upon it, and dreaming together. The vision was already planted in me [for Dream Builders], but I needed other believers to help me see the vision, to identify the voids and find the opportunities to plug in to fill these gaps in our ministry.

This panel of experts answered some of my other questions as well:

How do ordinary people dream God's dream?

1. Read God's word.
2. Hang around God's people.
3. Listen for God to speak through his people.
4. Listen for his voice.
5. Open yourself—say, "Here I am, Lord, send me."
6. Don't wait for the perfect time, perfect people, and perfect ministry before serving. Get in there and serve, and God will show you his dream. —*Lou*

Where do I find ministry opportunities?

I know this sounds funny, but they need to open their eyes. Too often we look for a bolt of lightning or writing across the sky, when we really need to open our eyes and look at the needs around us. As we see the needs, I believe they become our burning bush. —*Lou*

How do you take an idea deep within you and turn it into a reality?

First, I would encourage people to share their dream with someone they trust. Next, be patient and allow the dream to percolate and watch for doors to open. Open doors, to me, are usually seeing a real need for the ministry, other Christians who say "go for it," other people who want to be involved in the ministry, financial resources. Next, I would say, don't be afraid to fail. If it is God's plan, he will make it succeed (see Prov. 16:3). —*Lou*

What about failure?

Having the door slammed in your face is not always bad, however. At times I fall into the trap of dreaming my own dreams, and not God's dreams. I have grown [and learned about] changing challenges into positive experiences, so I knew nothing was impossible as we've ventured into our tutoring program. The tutoring program started slowly. It was from this small venture that we would later build the Clubhouse ministry. —*Mike*

The rhythm continues: God's initiative; my obedience. His plan within me; my response in action, no matter where the path may lead. God's plan for ministry; my call to fulfill that which is deep within me and to be God's hands and feet in the world.

We, lay and clergy alike, are in ministry together, following the agenda of Jesus to make him known and to lead his people to wholeness. This is the business of the church in renewal. (Appendix D provides a brief listing of the variety of ministries initiated and conducted at Ginghamsburg Church.)

It is the business of the church to help people identify God's burning bushes. Then we must throw gasoline, not water, on their burning bushes. Visions must be nurtured by leaders. We will explore this in greater depth in the next chapter.

Chapter VI

THE LEADERSHIP PRINCIPLE

Throughout history, God has always used a leader as change agent.
- Leadership and management are not the same.
- The leader understands and articulates the why (mission statement), the what (goal), and the how (strategy).

Do not neglect the gift that is in you, which was given to you through prophecy with the laying on of hands by the council of elders. Put these things into practice, devote yourself to them, so that all may see your progress. Pay close attention to yourself and to your teaching; continue in these things, for in doing this you will save both yourself and your hearers.

1 Timothy 4:14-16

The need was never so great. A chronic crisis of governance—that is, the pervasive incapacity of organizations to cope with the expectations of their constituents—is now an overwhelming factor worldwide. If there was ever a moment in history when a comprehensive strategic view of leadership was needed, not just by a few leaders in high office but by large numbers of leaders in every job, from the factory floor to the executive suite, from a McDonald's fast-food franchise to a law firm, this is certainly it.[1]

Warren Bennis and Burt Nanus

Often I hear the question, "What will happen to this church if Mike leaves? So much of what has happened at Ginghamsburg Church has been dependent on Mike's leadership."

My answer is, "Who knows what will happen? It depends on whether I'm followed by effective, anointed leadership."

There is a tendency to downplay the importance of leadership in the institutional church and to invalidate models of success in which a person is clearly identified as a catalyst. The system is confused by successful leaders. Who will replace them when they leave? Where do you send them? Leadership means change, and the system resists change. As Jesus observed, institutions tend to stone their prophets.

Throughout church history, there has been no example of renewal without a leader functioning as the catalyst. God has always used a human instrument as the agent for change. Abraham and Moses were the leaders associated with the old covenant and God's revelation through Judaism. God's promise of a unique people who would be priest to all nations was inspired through Abraham. The law that would mature and govern this people came through Moses.

Israel went through cycles of obedience, disobedience, repentance, and renewal. God would use judges like Deborah, reforming kings like Hezekiah or Josiah, and prophets as the instruments for renewal.

> [Hezekiah] was twenty-five years old when he became king.
> . . . He did what was right in the eyes of the LORD, just as his father David had done. He removed the high places, smashed the sacred stones and cut down the Asherah poles. He broke into pieces the bronze snake Moses had made, for up to that time the Israelites had been burning incense to it. Hezekiah trusted in the LORD, the God of Israel. There was no one like him among all the kings of Judah, either before him or after him. He held fast to the LORD and did not cease to follow him; he kept the commands the LORD had given Moses.
>
> (2 Kings 18:2*a*, 3-6 NIV)

These leaders would bring the people from their dead institutional-civil religion back into a vital covenant relationship with God. They inspired people to return to their first love.

Jesus and Paul are the leaders associated with God's revelation through the new covenant: "Do not think that I have come to abolish the Law or the Prophets; I have not come to abolish them but to fulfill them" (Matt. 5:17 NIV).

Jesus demonstrated the inner law of the renewed heart, rather than the rigid adherence to outward appearance through legalistic behavior. He was both the demonstration and the fulfillment of loving God with all one's heart, soul, and strength, and loving one's neighbor as oneself.

Paul's energies launched this localized Jewish movement globally: "For there is no difference between Jew and Gentile—the same Lord is Lord of all and richly blesses all who call on him, for, "Everyone who calls on the name of the Lord will be saved" (Rom. 10:13 NIV).

Paul's missionary journeys and writings brought God's message of reconciliation through his Son Jesus Christ to the "uttermost parts of the earth." It has affected kings and kingdoms, calendar systems, politics and the arts, education and social programs—all because God chooses to act and speak through human instruments.

The church also has experienced repeated cycles of obedience and disobedience. God has raised up leaders throughout history who have acted as reformers in calling the church back to her first love. In the fourth century, Augustine developed a systematic theology that helped give the church doctrinal stability in the midst of the rapidly growing cults. His work set a precedent for biblical integrity and trinitarian fidelity. His Christ-centered focus has influenced reformers' theology right up through the present time.

Luther was God's agent for renewal during the sixteenth century. The church had long since forgotten its first purpose. It had become a corrupt institutional bureaucracy that served the interest of the state, rather than the purpose of God.

Luther's posting of his Ninety-Five Theses on the door of the Castle Church in Wittenburg set in motion a revolution that cast off brittle wineskins. His bold leadership inspired new life and faith among the working-class people.

Ignatius Loyola, St. John of the Cross, and Teresa of Avila were God's agents in leading the Counter Reformation, the renewal movement in the Catholic Church, during that same time period.[2]

There has been a leader behind every awakening. John Calvin, and his emphasis on the sovereignty of God and divine election, further impacted Western Europe and the later Anabaptist movement. John Wesley's emphasis on individual responsibility, and his disciplined approach to discipleship, fueled the flames of renewal on two continents. Jonathan Edwards, Charles Finney, Billy Graham, and Mother Teresa—all have been God's agents to further the purpose of God's kingdom.

All movements have been inspired by great leaders. Gandhi inspired the passive-resistance movement that won India's freedom from Britain. Dr. Martin Luther King, Jr., empowered the civil-rights movement. Winston Churchill stepped forward to rally his nation's courage in resisting and holding off Nazi Germany. Japan's incredible economic turnaround in quality control was inspired by the post–World War II business pioneer, W. Edwards Deming.

What should be obvious must be stated. We cannot go forward without effective leadership. We cannot solve our present problems without effective leadership. Without effective leadership, we cannot promote necessary change.

For the church, the result is critically clear. Lack of leadership means decline and death. I have seen countless examples in which a healthy church loses a healthy leader, and then, under new pastoral direction, experiences significant decline in attendance and loss of focus. Not all leaders are equal, and even more significantly, most people in positions of leadership are not leaders! Leadership is not optional. The sheep need a shepherd.

A Critical Distinction

Leadership and management are not the same. Warren Bennis and Burt Nanus effectively clarify the difference:

> The problem with many organizations, and especially the ones that are failing, is that they tend to be overmanaged and underled. They may excel in the ability to handle the daily routine, yet never question whether the routine should be done at all. There is a profound difference between management and leadership, and both are important. "To manage" means "to bring about, to accomplish, to have charge of or responsibility for, to conduct." "Leading" is "influencing, guiding in direction, course, action, opinion." The distinction is crucial. *Managers are people who do things right and leaders are people who do the right thing.*[3]

The church is experiencing a major leadership crisis. We are skilled in the practice of century-old daily routines, but lack the vision, knowledge, and courage to do the right thing. We have many managers in the church but few leaders.

Leaders Are Driven Forward by Vision

Leaders are the people who have seen burning bushes. They have heard God's voice. They have a very clear picture in their minds of what God wants them to accomplish. Vision enables the leader to discern God's direction. It gives clarity of purpose. The leader is able to articulate clearly the "why" and "where," and speaks with the authority of God.

One of the best biblical examples contrasting the difference between leadership and management can be seen in Moses and Aaron. Moses had a clear "burning bush" experience—a vision from God:

> Then Moses went up to God, and the LORD called to him from the mountain and said, "This is what you are to say to the house of Jacob and what you are to tell the people of Israel" . . . . So

Moses went back and summoned the elders of the people and set before them all the words the LORD had commanded him to speak. (Exod. 19:3, 7 NIV)

Moses' revelation of the vision to the people leaves no sense that God's mandate is up for a vote.

The burning-bush experience is not as clear for the manager. Aaron was not on the mountain with Moses to hear God speak. He was more pastoral in his relationship with people, and more "hands on" in ministering to their needs. After all, Moses was never around when you really needed him. He would disappear for weeks at a time. He could have been accused of having his head in the clouds, of being withdrawn and distant—a dreamer!

Aaron, on the other hand, was always there. Many would consider him the ideal pastor. He didn't have the luxury of spare time to climb a mountain and find a burning bush. The people's needs were too pressing.

Because the manager lacks a clear vision, he or she becomes more of a facilitator of group process: "What do you think we should do?" "How do you feel about it?" "Where do you think we should be headed?" The group facilitator role, however, fails to take into account one very critical problem: It is in the nature of people to want to go back to Egypt. It doesn't matter that Egypt represents slavery. Egypt is all we have ever known. Here, Egypt represents the way we have always done it in the past. There is no freedom or opportunity in Egypt, but life there carries minimal risk and is predictable. After all, none of us have ever seen this "promised land" that Moses keeps talking about. What little information we have tells us that there are insurmountable obstacles. Some among us speak of giants that can never be overcome with our meager resources.

If you put it up for a vote, you will go back to Egypt! Or you will bring Egypt to you by building a golden calf in the wilderness. With very good intentions, that is exactly what Aaron does. Through the facilitation of group process, he enables the people to build a golden calf in God's name. He becomes the people's personal chaplain, managing their expectations by carrying on the sacred traditions that they have brought with them from Egypt. The manager does the expected thing. The leader is concerned with doing the *right* thing.

Never has this been more apparent to me than in the way we cling to outdated worship and music forms. I had just struggled through a highly liturgical, sparsely attended communion service. Even after six years of theological training, I had trouble making heads or tails of the experience.

Afterward, the pastor invited me for lunch. As we got in his car and headed out of the parking lot onto a suburban street, he apologized: "Communion Sunday is always a low attendance week."

I could not help noticing the booming housing developments all around his church. Young families were out in their yards, grilling, planting flowers, cutting grass, playing ball.

At his urging, I commented, "You will never reach those families if you don't change your worship style. Look at your own interest—you leave your radio tuned to an adult contemporary station."

He hesitated, loosened his tie, and then do you know what he said?

"I know it won't work. But that is what these people are used to. They have always done it this way. They will have to make up their minds to change if they want to grow."

I couldn't believe it! And I couldn't hold my tongue: "These people are not going to decide to change. They are in Egypt. Egypt is all they know. That is why you have been sent here. You are here to lead change. God has not sent you here to manage the expected thing. He did not give his Son for the purpose of maintaining the status quo. He sent Jesus to change it, and he has chosen you to be the leader."

A Leader's Dream Is Shaped by Others

So Elijah went from the there and found Elisha son of Shaphat. He was plowing with twelve yoke of oxen, and he himself was driving the twelfth pair. Elijah went up to him and threw his cloak around him. Elisha then left his oxen and ran after Elijah. "Let me kiss my father and mother good-by," he said, "and then I will come with you." (1 Kings 19:19-20 NIV)

God uses leaders to shape the dreams of leaders. Dr. King's vision for the civil-rights movement during the 1950s and 1960s was greatly influenced by Mahatma Gandhi's philosophy of leadership in the passive-resistance movement in India. John Wesley adopted his strategy of discipleship through cell groups from the Moravian leaders. George Whitefield influenced Wesley's method and style in field preaching.

Several "Bethlehem star" people and experiences have helped shape and clarify my own vision. Dietrich Bonhoeffer's *Cost of Discipleship* was one of the first books I read as a new Christian. From that point on, I would always see and proclaim the cost of what it means to be a follower of Jesus Christ. Grace must never be seen as "cheap," nor sold like cut-rate wares at the marketplace.

My experience in Campus Crusade for Christ at the University of Cincinnati evoked in me a strong commitment to systematic discipleship. Our Vital Christianity program for new members was influenced by my Campus Crusade years.

Dr. Ken Kinghorn, and his emphasis on the gifts of the Holy Spirit as the means to accomplish God's mission through the church, have affected my approach in choosing my own involvement in ministry, as well as influencing others. At Ginghamsburg, we use a spiritual-gifts inventory to help people decide where to become actively involved. My three years under Ken's influence during seminary forever shaped my understanding of empowerment for mission.

Tom Skinner was a radical influence in my life during the early 1970s. Through his ministry I saw the church as "God's new community on earth that modeled what was going on in heaven." The church is the community that "shows people what it is like when Jesus is in control." My commitment to blend a personal encounter with Jesus and social justice was shaped by my encounters with Tom Skinner.

Howard Snyder's books, *The Problem of Wineskins; Radical Wesley;* and *The Community of the King* have shaped my thinking and approach to strategy and church structures. Developing "new wineskins to hold new wine," and the emphasis on moving people from meetings to front-line mission, have evolved from his influence.

Don Joy, Mary Olson, Len Sweet, and others have thrown gasoline on my burning bush along the way. God uses Elijahs to shape the dreams of Elishas. Hanging out with the sold out enables one to more clearly dream God's dream.

> When the LORD was about to take Elijah up to heaven in a whirlwind, Elijah and Elisha were on their way from Gilgal. Elijah said to Elisha, "Stay here; the LORD has sent me to Bethel."
>
> But Elisha said, "As surely as the LORD lives and as you live, I will not leave you." So they went down to Bethel.
>
> (2 Kings 2:1-2 NIV)

Elisha knew that Elijah was a man who had heard God's voice. Whatever God had done for Elijah, or taught Elijah, Elisha wanted a double portion!

Seek out people of vision. Read whatever you can read. Ask questions. Go to seminars. During my early years at Ginghamsburg Church, I would travel to the Fuller Institute of Church Growth in Pasadena for seminars. We invited speakers like Juan Carlos Ortiz to come to our church. I would call effective pastors, to see if I could catch a glimpse of what God was showing them. As I write this chapter, I am preparing to go to Phoenix, Arizona, with my wife for a Leadership Network Conference. I have found that one of the best ways to see a burning bush is to find others who have seen one. Vision is contagious!

Leaders Are Focused on Results

Leaders begin with an end in mind. They have a clear picture of what the destination looks like before they begin the journey.

When I came to Ginghamsburg Church in April of 1979, I was very concerned with discovering God's mission for the church. I knew that this little country church had been in existence since 1863. And I also knew that each one of the ninety people involved would have an opinion of their own. At twenty-seven years of age, I sensed that my life and ministry was too short to be about anything less than the purpose of God. So I established, as my first priority, the ability to "see" God's purpose.

Throughout church history, leaders of renewal have been able to see beyond the immediate barriers of culture-bound tradition, to sense God's intent for purpose and direction.

On a chilly but sunny April morning, I went and stood in a field behind the little two-room church building—the site of our current discipleship center. Staring back at the modest church facility that looked like hundreds of others, I said: "Lord, I am not going to leave this field until I have a clear sense of your mission for this church."

Vision and the fortitude to accomplish God's purpose grow out of our willingness to wade out across the stream and wrestle with God. We need a willingness to wrestle and not let go until we have a sense of resolve about God's direction: "God, show me. I will not let go or turn back, if you assure me that you are with me."

We must first wrestle with God in our field of dreams if we are going to be able to speak to people with a sense of his authority. I prayed and I waited, for when we are sure that it is God's voice that we hear, we won't be so tempted to turn back during times of resistance.

I remained in the field for the rest of the afternoon. And as is so often the case, God speaks not through storm, fire, or earthquake, but through silence. His thoughts began to stream into my head. I could see three thousand people worshiping the Lord. A deep sense of God's feeling for the lost overwhelmed me. I am not a highly emotional person, but tears ran down my cheeks as I sensed God's pain for the people who lived thirty minutes in every direction from this building—people who had no understanding of his love and healing intention. That intention had to be made known. The resurrected Christ has the power to break addictions, overcome codependennt tendencies, and restore broken relationships. He is not about condemnation, but reconciliation.

I had a vision of a church that would be a teaching church, a place where ordinary people would come and be equipped to be fully assimilated and functioning members of the Body of Christ—disciples who would go out into the marketplace and win the lost; followers of Jesus who would be committed to work in the inner city in ministries to help set free the oppressed; people of compassion who would do lay counseling and develop support-group ministries. A picture of pastors and lay people coming to this place from other churches was forming in my spirit. They would come here to see what God was doing and take what they learned back to other churches, throughout our denomination and beyond, promoting renewal.

Standing knee-high in grass, I envisioned a ministry that would focus equally on a personal relationship with Christ and social action. God is not only a God who hurts for the lost, but one who also calls his people to be actively and aggressively involved in setting the oppressed free. (A reporter for the *Dayton Daily News* recently described Ginghamsburg as a church that "combines conservative evangelical theology with strong social activism.")

When I left the field it was late afternoon. I left with a sunburn and a clear sense of God's purpose, which has kept me moving forward and sustained me during my ministry at Ginghamsburg Church. This experience has been the basis for everything that has taken place. The power of vision enabled me to see the reality of God's success before it happened.

When a leader has a clear picture of God's destination, the people begin to articulate and live that vision. Over a period of time, that vision begins to penetrate the surrounding culture, and even the secular newspapers can identify and articulate the vision's objective.

Vision clarifies God's purpose and direction. When you clearly see God's purpose, any obstacles that come will pale in comparison.

Doing Things "By the Book"

While the leader focuses on the end result, the manager tends to focus on the method, or process. The manager wants to do things according to organizational expectations—to go "by the book."

In my denomination's structure, we have a yearly fall ritual of the nominating report. This form contains the many standardized offices and committees of the church. Managers rarely ask whether the labyrinth of committees is really needed to accomplish the mission of their particular church. They see it as their responsibility to "manage" the organizational structure. Many of our people end up wearing several different hats in the church, as we attempt to fill in all the slots. We challenge our people to become part of the greatest mission in the universe, and then place them on a committee in which they may do nothing more than argue over what kind of carpeting to put in the narthex.

I was recently invited to speak at a revival in a large church. The chair of the evangelism committee picked me up at the airport. When I asked her what her committee had accomplished during the previous twelve months, she told me that my coming to their church was a result of their labors. Twelve people met ten times for the sake of having me come? One person could have picked up the phone and called me. It would have involved a simple five-minute telephone conversation. See how many valuable people-hours were wasted!

Seventy percent of all baby-boomer women work outside the home. Many of them are single parents. By the time they pick up their children at day care and get the evening meal, they have very little time left to invest in a committee that accomplishes next to nothing. We must be very selective in choosing the ways we ask people to spend their lives.

We have not had an evangelism committee since I have been at Ginghamsburg Church. Evangelism is like breathing. It is the natural result of a healthy Body. Your physical body doesn't need a breathing committee to ask, "How are we going to breathe today?"

It is my goal to keep as few key leaders as possible in meetings and place the majority of them in the direct front-line of mission, reaching the lost and setting the oppressed free. I have found that many people who come home from work exhausted, and are consequently reluctant to give their time to committees, *are* willing to work in front-line mission that makes a difference in the lives of other people. They are willing to become involved in lay counseling programs, tutoring programs with children, support group and outreach ministries. These young working mothers and fathers are willing to give up Thanksgiving vacations to help rebuild homes for hurricane victims or serve dinner to the poor and lonely. They are willing to visit prisons and nursing homes, and serve God's purpose through a resale clothing store, food pantry, or furniture warehouse. People will give their time to answer telephones for crisis-intervention ministries.

We have been too busy to have an evangelism committee, or, for that matter, to fill many of the slots on the nominating form. Maybe someday we will have the time to get around to it, but then evangelism probably would stop. We must move people from meetings to mission.

Jesus did not ask us to join a committee. He chose us that we might go out and "bear fruit in his name." The structure of the church exists for this purpose. It is only a vehicle to accomplish the mission of Christ.

We have a tendency in the church to make our structures an end in themselves. They become sacred calves that we begin to worship and serve. Structures should never be seen as sacred institutions that never can be adapted, or even totally changed. They are temporary wineskins. Wineskins become brittle and need to be changed to hold next year's wine.

One structure that we tried to hold on to at Ginghamsburg Church was United Methodist Women. We tried for four years to make it work, but the young women we were attracting to our church did not relate to this wineskin. We had willingly changed all our other traditional structures, and they were working, but we had been unwilling to let go of this one ministry. United Methodist Women had become a golden calf.

My wife, Carolyn, got a group of women together and asked what kinds of ministry would appeal to them and best meet their needs. They began aerobics programs, craft classes, Bible studies, evening programs for working women, a resale clothing store, and annual retreats with national speakers. These ministries attract many unchurched women from the surrounding communities, and function from four to five days each week. The new wineskin is simply called "Women's Ministry." United Methodist Women has been a key strategy for mission in the past, but it must never become a golden calf. The leader sees the goal and is willing to change structures for the purpose of reaching that goal. Our goal is to accomplish the mission of Christ, not to serve the organizational structure. The structure must serve the goal.

The leader measures success by accomplishing right results, not by following the process of the structure.

The Leader Articulates the Vision

When I first came to Ginghamsburg Church, it was known as the chicken-noodle church. When I was introduced to several of the people in the community, I was met with the response, "Oh, you are the chicken-noodle pastor." For as long as anyone could remember, the church had focused its primary energies on two yearly chicken-noodle dinners.

The older women of the church would pass the tradition down to the younger women by telling them the sacred traditions of the chicken noodle. They would relate that in days gone by, the "god" mothers of the church would meet at the farmhouse next to the church, ring the chickens' necks, and pluck feathers. People would work for a month to get ready for the sacred feast. Noodles were rolled and cut, then placed on long tables in the basement of the church for drying and seasoning.

When the day of the sacred feast finally arrived, people from all over Miami County would drive to the little country church to participate in the renowned Ginghamsburg chicken-noodle dinner. Several hundred people would come. Every nook and cranny of this little church building was turned into a restaurant. People were served some of the best chicken noodles and homemade pies you ever tasted. When it was over, people relaxed, feeling a deep sense of accomplishment, only to remobilize later for the next feast.[4]

Is this what God had in mind when he chose the church to be his hands and feet in the world? The Son of God gave his life for dinners and bazaars? The Bible clearly states that "without a vision, the people perish." People need a challenging dream and a clearly defined purpose.

The leader is the one who is able to cast the dream. The leader must be able to answer the question about why we are here. The business of Christ is not about chicken-noodle dinners and bazaars. The business of Christ is about winning the lost and setting the oppressed free.

Clearly articulated visions are compelling. They attract people like magnets. Look at Dr. King's "I have a dream." I can still see him delivering that message from the steps of the Lincoln Memorial. His vision still lives within me, even though I was a young boy at the time.

Mike Nygren, our youth director at Ginghamsburg Church, is a dreamer. Incredible ministries have been born through people who catch fire from his dreams. Four Clubhouse ministries operate throughout the Dayton area—store-front ministries (missions) that work with children. The ministry includes tutoring in math and reading, field trips, kids' clubs, gymnastics, summertime recreation programs, and an annual camp. After school, middle-class teens from our church travel in vans to areas infested with crack dealers, to minister with children. Adults leave work early to work alongside the teens. As teens leave Mike's program for college, they take the vision with them. This year, Clubhouses were opened in Cincinnati and in Oxford, Ohio, with others being planned for Illinois and Indiana.

DreamBuilders is another of Mike's visions that draws teens and adults together for the purpose of building affordable, quality three-bedroom homes for financially stressed families. The team members begin framing the houses in the church parking lot, then truck them to their final destination for completion. Mike's team has already built three homes in the Appalachian area of southeastern Kentucky.

More than five hundred houses in the Dayton area have been insulated, in cooperation with the Dayton Power and Light Company, through Mike's original concept of the Dayton Work Project. President Bush personally presented Mike and Monica Stratman (a teen worker) with the 838th Point of Light Award for these ministries. President Clinton flew three of our people to the White House, to present them with The President's Volunteer Action Award. It is not hard to see why Mike has no trouble staffing his youth program with more than fifty adult counselors. Visions are compelling. People need a challenging vision and a clearly articulated purpose. They need to know that their lives and investments of time are making a real difference.

Tom Sager, our pastor of care and counseling, has been driven by God's dream of equipping laity to do basic counseling. More than one hundred Stephen ministers have been trained for caregiving through Tom's ministry. He also understood the need for professional counseling at affordable prices. How many people can afford counseling at $85 to $125 an hour? The people of Ginghamsburg church were caught up in Tom's vision and opened the New Creation Counseling Center. The center offers various support groups that deal with needs like eating disorders, chemical addictions, sexual abuse, and codependency. Five professional counselors and a support group specialist offer services from a Christian perspective, on a donation basis.

This is the business of Christ's church—winning the lost and setting the oppressed free! The leader is able to effectively communicate that business. A clearly articulated vision motivates and energizes people. The leader understands that the people need energy, vision, and direction more than program management. As Elisha said to Elijah, "I want a double portion of the Spirit that is in you."

The Leader Clarifies the Mission: Why Are We Here?

If I went into the corporate offices of Coca Cola Bottling Company in Atlanta, Georgia, and asked anyone, from the janitor to the CEO, what the company's mission is, they would be able to give me a very clear, succinct answer—to sell Coca Cola. They have been very effective in accomplishing their mission. Everywhere I have traveled throughout the world, from the most populated cities to remote villages without electricty, I have found Coca Cola. I was preaching in a rural village in India on the day electricity first reached that area in 1975. They had yet to experience electricity, but they knew well the taste of Coke.

When I ask the leaders of our churches the same question— "What is your mission?"—their answers do not have the same clarity of purpose. If the church were as diligent as the Coca Cola Bottling Company, this world would be evangelized.

Furniture Warehouse

The Furniture Warehouse provides used furniture to those in need and enables the members of Ginghamsburg Church to share their abundance with others. The Warehouse accepts furniture from many sources, refurbishes it, and distributes it with love, with no obligation to those in need. Also, Warehouse volunteers regularly load a truck with excess clothing and furniture, and deliver the items to distribution locations in Appalachia.

H.E.L.P.

The Home Environment Labor Partners concept allows our members to provide assistance for maintenance needs and daily tasks to those who are elderly, disabled, widowed, or in financial stress. These tasks include minor home repair, auto maintenance, painting, and other services.

Love Fund

Members of Ginghamsburg Church can receive financial and material assistance as required, in time of temporary crisis or unusual situations. This is a way we can share what Jesus has given us with others in our Body. A need expressed is all that is required. This fund is designed to overcome those difficult times with dignity.

New Creation Counseling Center

New Creation Counseling Center seeks to respond to persons in pain. Through our counselors, our Stephen Ministers, and our support groups, we offer distinctively Christian support and healing. Because we believe Jesus Christ is the ultimate answer to our needs, we want to help people grow in their relationships with Christ and, in particular, to apply his healing presence and love at the point of their needs. We understand that this is neither a simple nor a magical procedure, but rather a gradual and profound process of moving further into spiritual and emotional wholeness through Christ.

The New Creation Counseling Center has its own facility. At present, more than 35 Stephen ministers and four professional counselors lead the ministry endeavors. The center is under the direction of a full-time pastor, who has responsibility for care and counseling at Ginghamsburg church.

Nursing Home Ministry

Our nursing-home outreach seeks to connect the people within the church with the nursing home residents, by offering companionship, love, care, and sharing of God's Word in worship and song. We also provide large-print Bibles and offer Bible study, both individually and in small-groups. Our intent is to provide ongoing relationship and caring.

Prison Ministry

Persons involved in the prison ministry witness to inmates through friendship, time, love, and gifts. We seek to lift up people in despair and loneliness by providing them with the Lord's Word and the actions of caring Christians. A central part of the ministry is the pen-pal program, which links the inmates with someone outside the prison.

Women's Center

This is a Christian Pro-life outreach to the community and abortion alternative center. This ministry provides counseling, support, and sharing of the Word, while maintaining the client's anonymity. Pregnancy testing also is offered with no charge or obligation. The center is self-supporting.

Appendix D

Preschool Ministry

Currently, 95 children participate in our 5-day-a-week preschool program. About 80 percent of these 3- to 5-year-old children come from unchurched families.

NOTES

Introduction

1. Richard E. Wilke, *And Are We Yet Alive?* (Nashville: Abingdon Press, 1986), p. 26.
2. Major periods of growth and renewal: New Testament Church and its rapid missionary expansion before it was legalized under Constantine, 313 A.D.; the conversion of St. Augustine and his influence over the church, 4th century; the Reformation and Counter Reformation in the Catholic Church, 1517–1648; the Wesleyan Renewal, 18th century; the two Great Awakenings in American history—under Jonathan Edwards, 18th century, and under Charles Finney, 19th century. The current renewal is seen throughout various pockets of the church and expressed in various forms, like the charismatic movement and the rapid growth of the church in third-world countries.
3. Story used with permission of Bill and Norma Stout, faithful servants in Christ's mission at Ginghamsburg United Methodist Church.
4. William G. McLoughlin, "Revivalism," in *The Rise of Adventism*, ed. Edwin Scott Gaustad (New York: Harper & Row, 1974), p. 132.

1. The Lordship Principle

1. Lyle E. Schaller, "What Happened to Denominations," *The Clergy Journal* (October 1992), pp. 45-47.
2. Jurgen Moltmann, *The Way of Jesus Christ: Christology in Messianic Dimensions* (New York: Harper Collins, 1990), p. 41.
3. Hugh T. Kerr and John M. Mulder, *Conversions: The Christian Experience* (Grand Rapids: Eerdmans, 1983), p. 11.
4. F. J. Foakes-Jackson, *History of the Christian Church to A.D. 461* (Chicago: W. P. Blessing, 1927), pp. 494, 495.
5. A. G. Dickens, *The Counter Reformation* (Great Britain: Harcourt, Brace & World, 1969), p. 37.
6. Roland Bainton, *Here I Stand: A Life of Martin Luther* (Nashville: Abingdon Press, 1950), p. 60.
7. A. G. Dickens, *The Counter Reformation* (Great Britain: Harcourt, Brace & World, 1969), p. 7.
8. Ibid., pp. 77, 80.

9. *The Journal of John Wesley, A. M.*, ed. Nehemiah Curnock (New York: Eaton & Mains, 1909), pp. 471-72.
10. Ibid., pp. 475-76.
11. Ibid., pp. 477-78.
12. Robert W. Burtner and Robert E. Chiles, *A Compend of Wesley Theology* (Nashville: Abingdon Press, 1954), p. 73.

2. The Biblical Principle

1. Robert W. Burtner and Robert E. Chiles, *A Compend of Wesley's Theology* (Nashville: Abingdon Press, 1954), p. 21.
2. Ibid., pp. 20, 21.
3. Robert E. Chiles, *Scriptural Christianity: A Call to John Wesley's Disciples* (Grand Rapids: Zondervan, 1984), p. 70.
4. A. G. Dickens, *The Counter Reformation* (Great Britain: Harcourt, Brace & World, 1969), p. 160.

3. The Liturgical Principle

1. Leonard Sweet, *First Love*. 1990. Produced and directed by Michael Slaughter. 90 min. Media Resources for Ministry at United Theological Seminary. Videocassette.
2. Louis F. Benson, *The Hymnody of the Christian Church* (New York: George H. Doran Co., 1927), pp. 240-41.
3. Kenneth G. Phifer, *A Protestant Case for Liturgical Renewal* (Philadelphia: Westminster Press, 1965), p. 98.
4. Ibid., p. 103.

4. The Covenant Principle

1. Howard Snyder, *First Love*. 1990. Produced and directed by Michael Slaughter. 90 min. Media Resources for Ministry at United Theological Seminary. Videocassette.
2. Robert E. Chiles, *Scriptural Christianity: A Call to John Wesley's Disciples* (Grand Rapids: Zondervan, 1984), p. 75.

5. The Priesthood Principle

1. Leonard Sweet, *First Love*.1990. Produced and directed by Michael Slaughter. 90 min. Media Resources for Ministry at United Theological Seminary. Videocassette.

6. The Leadership Principle

1. Warren Bennis and Burt Nanus, *Leaders: The Strategies for Taking Charge* (New York: Harper & Row, 1985), p. 2.

2. The name "Counter Reformation" seems inappropriate, in the sense that the movement was renewing faith and focus in the Catholic Church, not countering what the Protestant reformers were doing.
3. Bennis and Nanus, *Leaders,* p. 21.
4. There was one other yearly event—the annual Christmas Bazaar. People would spend from July until November making crafts to raise money for mission. A bazaar is not the most efficient use of time or resources to raise money for mission. It is much more effective to just take the money from our pockets to serve Christ's purpose.
5. George Barna, *The Frog in the Kettle* (Ventura, Calif.: Regal Books, 1990), p. 142.

Appendix B

1. *The Works of John Wesley, Volume VIII, Addresses, Essays, Letters* (Grand Rapids: Baker Book House, 1978), pp. 272-74.

BIBLIOGRAPHY

ANDERSON, James D., and JONES, Ezra Earl.
  1986   *Ministry of the Laity.* San Francisco: Harper & Row.

ANDERSON, Leith.
  1992   *A Church for the 21st Century.* Minneapolis: Bethany House.
  1990   *Dying for Change.* Minneapolis: Bethany House.

ARN, Win, and ARN, Charles.
  1982   *The Master's Plan for Making Disciples.* Pasadena: Church Growth Press.

BAINTON, Roland.
  1950   *Here I Stand: A Life of Martin Luther.* Nashville: Abingdon Press.

BARNA, George.
  1992   *The Barna Report 1992–93.* Ventura, Calif.: Regal Books.
  1992   *Church Marketing.* Ventura, Calif.: Regal Books.
  1990   *The Frog in the Kettle.* Ventura, Calif.: Regal Books.
  1992   *The Power of Vision.* Ventura, Calif.: Regal Books.
  1993   *Turn-Around Churches.* Ventura, Calif.: Regal Books.
  1991   *User Friendly Churches.* Ventura, Calif.: Regal Books.

BONHOEFFER, Dietrich.
  1949   *The Cost of Discipleship.* New York: MacMillan.

BURTNER, Robert W., and CHILES, Robert E.
  1954   *A Compend of Wesley's Theology.* Nashville: Abingdon Press.

CALLAHAN, Kennon L.
  1983   *Twelve Keys to an Effective Church: Strategic Planning for Mission.* San Francisco: Harper & Row.

Bibliography

CHANEY, Charles L., and LEWIS, Ron S.
  1977   *Design for Church Growth*. Nashville: Broadman Press.

CHILES, Robert E.
  1984   *Scriptural Christianity: A Call to John Wesley's Disciples.*
          Grand Rapids: Zondervan.

CHO, Paul Yonggi.
  1984   *More Than Numbers*. Dallas: Word Books.
  1984   *Prayer: Key to Revival*. Dallas: Word Books.

COLEMAN, Robert E.
  1963   *The Master Plan of Evangelism*. Old Tappan, N. J.: Fleming
          H. Revell.

CURNOCK, Nehemiah, ed.
  1909   *The Journal of John Wesley, A.M.* New York: Eaton &
          Mains.

DEPREE, Max.
  1989   *Leadership Is an Art*. New York: Doubleday Dell.
  1992   *Leadership Jazz*. New York: Bantam Doubleday Dell.

DESCHNER, John
  1960   *Wesley's Christology*. Dallas: Southern Methodist University
          Press.

DICKENS, A. G.
  1969   *The Counter Reformation*. Great Britain: Harcourt, Brace
          & World.

EIMS, Leroy.
  1978   *The Lost Art of Disciple Making*. Grand Rapids: Zondervan.

ELLER, Vernard.
  1980   *The Outward Bound: Caravaning as the Style of the Church.*
          Grand Rapids: Eerdmans.

FOAKES-JACKSON, F. J.
  1927   *History of the Christian Church to A.D. 461*. Chicago: W. P.
          Blessing.

GALLAWAY, Ira.
  1983   *Drifted Away: Returning the Church to Witness and Min-
          istry*. Nashville: Abingdon Press.

Bibliography

GAUSTAD, Edwin Scott, ed.
1974   *The Rise of Adventism*. New York: Harper & Row.

GEORGE, Carl F.
1993   *How to Break Growth Barriers*. Grand Rapids: Baker Book House.
1991   *Prepare Your Church for the Future*. Grand Rapids: Fleming H. Revell.

GREEN, Hollis L.
1972   *Why Churches Die: A Basic Guide to Evangelism and Church Growth*. Minneapolis: Bethany Fellowship.

HUNTER, George G. III.
1979   *The Contagious Congregation*. Nashville: Abingdon Press.
1992   *How to Reach Secular People*. Nashville: Abingdon Press.
1987   *To Spread the Power: Church Growth in the Wesleyan Spirit*. Nashville: Abingdon Press.

JOHNSON, Douglas W., and WALTZ, Alan K.
1987   *Facts and Possibilities: An Agenda for The United Methodist Church*. Nashville: Abingdon Press.

KELLY, Dean M.
1972   *Why Conservative Churches Are Growing*. New York: Harper & Row.

KERR, Hugh T., and MULDER, John M., eds.
1983   *Conversions: The Christian Experience*. Grand Rapids: Eerdmans.

McCLOUGHLIN, William G.
1978   *Revivals, Awakenings, and Reform: An Essay on Religion and Social Change in America 1607–1977*. Chicago: University Press.

McGAVRAN, Donald A.
1980   *Understanding Church Growth*, Rev. Ed. Grand Rapids: Eerdmans.

McGAVRAN, Donald, and ARN, Winfield C.
1973   *How to Grow a Church*. Glendale, Calif.: Regal Books.
1977   *Ten Steps for Church Growth*. San Francisco: Harper & Row.

1981   *Back to Basics in Church Growth*. Wheaton, Ill.: Tyndale House.

McGAVRAN, Donald, with HUNTER, George; ed. Lyle Schaller
1980   *Church Growth: Strategies That Work*. Nashville: Abingdon Press.

MARTIN, Glen, and GINTER, Dian.
1994   *Power House: A Step-By-Step Guide to Building a Church That Prays*. Nashville: Broadman Press.

MILLER, Herb, with SCHALLER, Lyle.
1987   *How to Build a Magnetic Church*. Nashville: Abingdon Press.

MOLTMANN, Jurgen.
1990   *The Way of Jesus Christ: Christology in Messianic Dimensions*. New York: Harper Collins.

NEWBIGIN, Lesslie.
1986   *Foolishness to the Greeks: The Gospel and Western Culture*. Grand Rapids: Eerdmans.
1989   *The Gospel in a Pluralist Society*. Grand Rapids: Eerdmans.

NICHOLS, James Hastings.
1968   *Corporate Worship in the Reformed Tradition*. Philadelphia: Westminster Press.

O'CONNOR, Elizabeth
1963   *Call to Commitment*. New York: Harper & Row.
1968   *Journey Inward, Journey Outward*. New York: Harper & Row.

PHIFER, Kenneth G.
1965   *A Protestant Case for Liturgical Renewal*. Philadelphia: Westminster Press.

RAINER, Thom S.
1993   *The Book of Church Growth: History, Theology, and Principles*. Nashville: Broadman Press.

ROOZEN, David A., and HARDAWAY, C. Kirk.
1993   *Church and Denominational Growth*. Nashville: Abingdon Press.

Bibliography

SCHALLER, Lyle E.
1987   *It's a Different World*. Nashville, Abingdon Press.
1985   *The Middle-Sized Church*. Nashville: Abingdon Press.
1983   *Growing Plans: Strategies to Increase Your Church's Membership*. Nashville: Abingdon Press.

SNYDER, Howard A.
1977   *The Community of the King*. Downer's Grove, Ill.: Inter-Varsity Press.
1976   *The Problem of Wineskins: Church Structure in a Technological Age*. Downer's Grove, Ill.: Intervarsity Press.
1980   *The Radical Wesley and Patterns for Church Renewal*. Downer's Grove, Ill.: InterVarsity Press.

STEDMAN, Ray C.
1972   *Body Life*. Glendale, Calif.: Regal Books.

SWEET, Leonard.
1994   *Faithquakes*. Nashville: Abingdon Press.

TILLAPAUGH, Frank F.
1982   *The Church Unleashed: Getting God's People Out Where the Needs Are*. Ventura, Calif.: Regal Books.

TRUEBLOOD, Elton.
1980   *The Company of the Committed*. San Francisco: Harper & Row.

VAUGHAN, John N.
1985   *The Large Church: A Twentieth-Century Expression of the First-Century Church*. Grand Rapids: Baker Book House.

WAGNER, C. Peter.
1984   *Leading Your Church to Growth*. Ventura, Calif.: Regal Books.
1987   *Strategies for Church Growth*. Ventura, Calif.: Regal Books.
1976   *Your Church Can Grow: Seven Vital Signs of a Healthy Church*. Glendale, Calif.: Regal Books.

WAGNER, C. Peter, ed., with ARN, Win, and TOWNS, Elmer.
1986   *Church Growth, State of the Art*. Wheaton, Ill.: Tyndale House.

Bibliography

WATSON, David Lowes.
1987   *The Early Methodist Class Meeting: Its Origins and Significance.* Nashville: Discipleship Resources.

WESTERHOFF, John H. III.
1985   *Living the Faith Community: The Church That Makes a Difference.* San Francisco: Harper & Row.

WILKE, Richard E.
1986   *And Are We Yet Alive?* Nashville: Abingdon Press.

WILLIMON, William H., and WILSON, Robert L.
1987   *Rekindling the Flame: Strategies for a Vital United Methodism.* Nashville: Abingdon Press.